CLUELESS IN PARADISE

CLUELESS IN PARADISE
And Collected Essays

Sam Culotta

Copyright © 2020 Sam R. Culotta
All rights reserved.
ISBN-13:978-179537-943-4

Dedicated to Terri.. the one, the only

CONTENTS

Part One

1 Radio Street Days

7 Puppy Dog Tails

11 The Visit

18 Blue Collar Limousine

24 A Movin' And A Groovin

34 Mangiare Di Tutto

39 An Accidental Education

47 Yearbook Therapy

53 Christmas Eve, 1961

61 Temporary Quarters

70 Oh, The Waters

75 No Sweat

81 Captain Contrary

88 How I learned To Speak Italian Incorrectly

101 I Sing The Body Decrepit

106 Herbert J. Moriarity

112 Bathrooms

117 Footsies

123 Gift Wrapped With Love

Part Two

129 Poison

134 Groupings

139 Et Tu, Santa?

144 Look At It This Way

154 John Cameron Swayze's Camel News Caravan

162 Teach A Man To Fish

168 Pity The Poor Pessimist

176 Among The Humans

182 Authors Anonymous

200 The End Of The Beginning

209 List Of Books, Stories and Phrases Important To My Life

218 Clueless In Paradise

PREFACE

Those readers familiar with my previous book, Sleeping With Lumbago, will recognize the tone and point of view of the essays in Part One. During and after the publication of that book I continued to write pieces in the "Often Humorous, Always Personal Essays" style indicated by SLW's subtitle. Indeed, most of the pieces in this book could be characterized in the same way.

Part Two introduces essays that differ in tone and purpose. Most are unabashed opinion pieces, others are departures into territory I'm not certain of myself. A few are experimental, particularly "The End of the Beginning" and "List of The Books, Stories And Phrases Important To My Life".

The book closes with the title piece "Clueless In Paradise", a sort of travel piece about my recent trip to Sicily with my sister, Patti Amesbury.

Notes:

"Christmas Eve 1961" first appeared in the e magazine, ` "The Write Place At The Write Time", and again in "Into The Past", co-authored with Tim Smith and Joe Green.

"Radio Days" appears in "Into The Past".

PART ONE

Radio Street Days

"Four days! Four long days, I pushed and pushed but you wouldn't come out! Four days of labor! It was like my bones were cracking. So, the doctor decided to use tools to pull you out. You were long, 21 inches, but skinny. You weighed only six and a half pounds, all bones sticking out everywhere. That's why your rib is that way. The doctor said you had Rickets, caused by calcium deficiency. I couldn't drink milk when I was carrying you because it made me sick. But you were beautiful to me. You were my beautiful son. Dad was so proud he drove to the Gianfortti's house and threw stones at their bedroom window to wake them up. It was early in the morning because you were born at twelve-thirty A.M. Johnny, your Godfather to be, opened the window and dad shouted: 'I have a son! I have a son!' Oh, he was so proud."

And so I was born, in a hospital next to a blooming lilac grove. My mother told me this story more than once. One time she told it to me in front of my friends whose mother was playing cards with her at our house. She was a little bit "happy" from wine. But, really, how many of us know this much about their birth? It will come in handy should I ever write an autobiography.

There's a picture of me on Emmet Street. I'm maybe three and I'm in a driveway, sitting in a pedal car, hands on the little steering wheel, looking at the camera, a Kodak box camera held by my mother no doubt. (The shutter mechanism in those early boxes made an echoing sound that suggested its name to George Eastman: Ko-Dak.) We lived in an apartment when I was small. I don't think we were there very long before my parents bought their first home on Radio Street. My memories of Emmet Street don't even include the scene in the photograph. They are vague, dream-like: the ferny tops of plants, probably fennel.

    A few doors down the street lived some *comáre* or other whom Mom would visit from time to time. A member of their family died and I remember going there with her to express condolences over coffee "*and*". After that, not much. I did throw a pebble at a passing car once. The driver stopped and brought me to my mother who punished me later.

Radio Street occupied a more important and vivid segment of my youth. The first kid I met was a big boy about two years my senior. He became my first friend, if you count someone who alternately played with you and bullied you, a friend. Joe was his name, Joey Hause. It was mostly a German-American neighborhood with only one Italian family, ours, and one Jewish family, the Brauns. David Braun became one of my best friends. His family were the first in our immediate area to get a television and his mother was nice enough to let a few of us watch it most afternoons. Only a test pattern and news strip which ran along the bottom for the first half hour or so. The news was about the Korean War: how many of them we had killed, how many of ours had died, what river or bridge we had crossed, how much territory we had won or lost.

    "The Howdy Doody Show" began the day's programming. We loved Clarabelle the clown, we booed Phineas T. Bluster. show ended we went home to our dinner a happy bunch.

Clueless In Paradise

    David's teenage sister didn't like us being around. She was not friendly at all and complained about everything we did. In snowy weather she would put her boots on the rug outside their apartment door. One day I snuck up the stairs and lit her boot laces on fire. She got screaming mad when she saw them but couldn't prove who did it. Young boys have their own code of justice.
    I led what passed for a neighborhood gang, all of us in third or fourth grade. We did things like travel all the way up the street through backyards. Some yards had wooden fences, some had dogs some had mean old ladies, some had all three. It was a daunting excursion and it required nerve, agility and a degree of ingenuity. We also conducted raids on a neighbor's garden and stored our booty in a buried metal box. I guess we should have eaten it, but then we wouldn't have had the booty. If activities like this could earn you a merit badge I might have been a success in Cub Scouts. As it was, I managed to last just long enough to attend the annual Cub Scout picnic where my pals and I were inducted to exalted the rank of "Tenderfoot" I couldn't stand the regimentation and really sucked at braiding.
    My short stay in the Scouts was the beginning of a lifelong inability to stay aligned with any scholastic or social organization. A short time after my Tenderfoot career, I was forced to attend Turner's Gym. My Godmother's son was a member and my mother felt it would be a good experience for me. A few weeks of going there only to suffer the humiliation of standing naked on the stairs while the big boys came up from the indoor swimming pool laughing and snapping their wet towels at our private areas, was enough. Not to mention the bus ride home in the gathering dark.

Sam Culotta

If you can remember staying home sick from school you might remember how the afternoon hours weighed down on you like a hundred pounds of wet steel-wool. The mornings were nice; you had the sudden sense of freedom. By noon the buzz began to wear off, and by one or two the radio soap operas came on. As my mother ironed, I was forced to hear boring stories, the saccharine organ music and, the soap commercials: "Duz does it!", Use Ajax, the foaming cleanser. Floats the dirt, right down the drain!" "Ivory Soap, ninety-nine one hundredth's percent pure." And there was the smell of the hot iron. It all forms a sensory memory as melancholy as it is nostalgic. I still don't like afternoons.

On the next street there was a dairy. In that dairy was a little store that sold dairy products including ice cream bars and frozen Snicker's. And on a table behind the counter was a basket filled with farm fresh eggs. On the corner of our street and Clinton Avenue there was a movie theater: the Empress. And in the Empress was a ticket booth with a window facing our street. The window was covered by an open-wire screen to protect against flying rocks. Armed with stolen farm fresh eggs, we would tap on the screen to get the ticket seller's attention, then throw the eggs against the window and run like hell.

It was a short walk from our house to St. Michael's, a grand, gothic revival style Catholic church topped by a large cross of gold. Not real gold, I'm sure, but shiny and rich looking anyway. It soars almost three hundred feet into the sky and you can see it from a long distance away. I found a certain comfort in seeing it when I was away from our neighborhood. There was talk of St. Michael's having been considered as home to the local Bishop thus earning it the designation of cathedral. It was dedicated in 1892, almost twenty years before Sacred Heart Cathedral, but Sacred Heart was constructed for the purpose of housing the diocesan Bishop. St. Michael's parish was in a lower middle-class part of the city; Sacred Heart was planted in the wealthier part of the city, the part where George Eastman once lived and which now houses the Eastman House with its Kodak museum.

I don't know to this day how my parents with their limited resources managed to afford it, but they sent me to St. Michael's Catholic School. I attended classes there from the first through the seventh grades after which my father moved our family across country to Southern California. My mother was not thrilled and her family even less so. Grandma Lafranca called him a "somnabitch" as we pulled out of her driveway and headed out. Six months later she was living with us, so I'd say she got in the last lick.

My mother, my sister, Grandma and I returned for a visit two years later. I took one long walk to Radio Street with the same boy who shared my Turner's Gym experience. It hadn't changed. My real goal was to visit Critic's Ice Cream Parlor around the corner on Clinton Avenue a short block beyond the Empress Theater with its wire-screened ticket window. I knew Critics was where the kids from school hung out. Sure enough, a few were there including a girl who sent me heartfelt letters when we moved away. She, apparently, *had* changed. We exchanged a few pleasantries and she left with her friends. *Sic transit amour.*

It would be another forty-three before we returned.

Sam Culotta

This time, my uncle agreed to take my wife and me to Radio Street on the proviso that we remain in the car, look from the street and not stay long. "White Flight" and urban blight had turned my old neighborhood into a dangerous place. Strangers in suspicious cars, like my uncle's shiny Cadillac, were cause for discomfort. I noticed a few curtains being moved aside. Little about the house of my youth had changed. The small front porch with its shabby railing which I sat astride as my sadistic friend from next door pounded my leg, was still there. The graying shingles looked like the originals but could not have been. I couldn't tell if my beloved Bartlett pear tree was still there in the back yard.. In late summer it dropped swollen fruit that burst on the ground and gathered bees and ants. I knew I would be pushing my luck to ask to get out and check. The engine was running and my uncle's foot was getting twitchy, so off we went.

Postscript

We visited Rochester again recently to honor my Uncle Mike, (same uncle), on his ninetieth birthday. Aside from him, I am now the oldest male in my family. This is to say, most of the families descended from my parents are of a younger generation than mine now. I am sorry to report, however, that the urban vs. suburban social malady appears little changed. Sometimes, you can go home again.

Puppy Dog Tails

I'm not a Luddite, nor am I a "techie". I am reasonably tech savvy yet I cling to a certain amount of nostalgia for bygone ways. This was brought home to me when I read the Charley Brown strip in this morning's paper. The teacher chose Charley Brown to beat out the erasers. The joke was that when he had finished he was encrusted in chalk dust. Mildly amusing at best but oh so sweetly reminiscent of my own school days. The modern white board certainly makes things easier; the markers are cheap enough and they wipe away easily with an eraser that closely resembles what we used.

Charley's haven been "chosen" to perform the task speaks volumes. Back in the day", a phrase that wore itself out long ago, the boards were black slate and the chalk was white and the dust was omnipresent. The nuns in our school always carried the evidence of their occupation on some part of their flowing black habits. Fingers were coated with the stuff, noses were caked with it, eyes were attacked by it, and our poor little underdeveloped lungs probably wore it like wallpaper. Beating the dust out of erasers was a dirty job, but that was the least of it. Two classes of students were assigned this after school task: miscreants and teachers' pets. The former earned their shame the latter earned their brownie points. The former were teased by their pals who surely had been in the same place at one time or more, while the latter were ridiculed by the boys for being "goodie-goodies". The former were always boys, the latter were almost always girls

Occasionally there would be a boy shameless enough to volunteer thereby setting the tone for the rest of his time at school. The nuns made no effort to disguise their dislike for boys. We were dirty, unkempt, mischievous, profane and just plain disgusting. The girls were spared the slaps and ruler whacks Sister handed out to the boys with a certain amount of righteous anger. I was slapped for turning my head in church, for answering the girl in front of me who turned to speak to me in class, for goofing around on my way back to my desk after recess. The most unjust of many injustices came one day after I had returned from lunch.

Most of us lived nearby the school and were allowed to go home for lunch. On this particular day there had been a fresh snowfall; a gift to rival the manna that fell onto Moses' starving refugees in the desert. Sister recognized the exuberance building in her male charges. True to her calling she knew it was her duty to crush our childish joy just in case it led to us having fun.

"Children, before I release you to go home to lunch let me make one thing perfectly clear. You boys are not to make snowballs or to engage in snowball throwing" Then she added with great emphasis: " Is that understood?"

"Yes, Sister", we intoned robotically.

We ran outside to find the lawns covered with a delicious blanket of fresh snow just moist enough to make packing it irresistible. Well, not that irresistible; we had Sister's dire warning still ringing in our ears. When a couple of my "home boys" and I turned the corner onto our street we saw a group of guys, non-Catholics, one and all, making snowballs with gay abandon. When they saw us they formed into a battle unit and quickly turned against us with a vengeance and began pelting us with snowballs solid enough to hurt. One of them hit my friend in the side of the head and he went King Kong nuts. What else could we do but rush to the aid of our fallen brother?

Sister's threat vanished in the fog of war and we engaged the enemy with righteous fury. Besides, we were standing on my lawn and a guy should be able to make snowballs on his own lawn, right? Wrong.

We returned from lunch, removed our boots and jackets and resumed our assigned seats when Sister stepped into the room. She stood before us in silence; never a good sign.

"The following boys come up here and line up side by side."

She then read off the names of three of us, myself included. One by one we left our seats and trudged forward like dead men walking and lined ourselves up. Sister's face was undergoing physiological change before our eyes. Her wimple-smooshed cheeks took on a rosy hue while her eyes lost their normally grey cast to become something more akin to hot lead. (In retrospect, I think she was getting some sort of forbidden pleasure from this.)

"Now, I'm told that you boys saw fit to ignore my instructions and, in fact, not only made snowballs but even engaged in a snowball fight on your way home." She said.

I began to explain about how we were attacked and had to defend ourselves.

"Enough!'

"But, I was on my own.. "

"Enough, I said! Turn and face the wall."

She proceeded then to do violence to our respective derrieres with a yardstick.

"Now, return to your seats. I hope you learned your lesson."

Sure it hurt, but what hurt worse was hearing the girls giggle. We knew that one of them had seen us and had squealed. Sister was judge, jury and executioner. And we were, after all, boys.

That afternoon while we were beating the erasers and choking on chalk dust, we groused about how unfair it all was. And we tried to figure which of the girls had ratted on us and how we could get even with her. We had a pretty good idea who it was but we knew we weren't going to exact revenge. You can't get even with girls any more than you can get even with nuns.

The Visit

It began with the annual summer ritual of going to the train station to pick up my grandfather who was arriving from New York City. Rochester's New York Central Station, as it was called then, was the local depot for the eponymous train itself. It was one of those classic testaments to the glory and romance of train travel. I've been in more than a few over the years and they share the same majestic aura; expanses of marble and tile floors, ensconced lights on gilt-decorated walls that reach up to vaulted ceilings that echo voices and the sounds of luggage trolleys. And when the doors open out, the teasing scent of diesel from waiting cabs and idling locomotive engines wafts in.

    We were excited waiting for Grandpa's arrival; we didn't get many visitors so his was a novelty, and it marked the beginning of a festive two weeks during which I shucked off the name, Roger, (given to me by my father to cloak my obvious Sicilian features should I ever apply for work at Eastman Kodak or Bausch and Lomb; it was war time), and donned Sam out of respect for my namesake who might be insulted to hear me referred to by my middle name. In retrospect, I believe this was genuine excitement, not the sort children feel now because they know that visiting grandparents and aunts and uncles are sure to have some sort of treasure for them hidden in their luggage. My grandfather brought nothing but two worn, tan and brown striped suitcases, one of which

I was commissioned to lug to the car.

During his stay, our only grandfather/grandson adventure was a walk up Radio Street to the barber shop on nearby Clinton Ave. where we would get our hair cut for the whopping price of fifty cents, his treat. While he was in the chair I perused the National Geographic magazines for pictures of naked native women. That was about it until evening when the real action began.

Our family gathered dutifully every night, usually at our house. My parents were the eldest children of their parents and so our home was both resting and gathering place for everyone. I loved it because my cousins, two boys and a girl, were over most times and we could run rampant while the adults were busy drinking, laughing, swearing, bitching, and generally behaving like Sicilians. The men sat in the backyard under the pear tree with cold bottles of Standard Ale or Genesee Beer. The dark was festooned by the red-tips of Luckies, Camels, Pall Malls, Chesterfields and a riot of fireflies. Grandpa held the seat of honor.

Inside, the women sat and socialized. In their midst was Grandma, whom Grandpa had walked out on many years earlier, leaving her, my father, his six younger brothers and sisters, and a healthy dose of resentment behind. People of his generation didn't run out on their marriages; they toughed them out no matter what the cost, but he was lured to New York City by a friend who promised him work which turned out to be janitorial work in a high-rise building. "Sam, Sam the lavatory man", they would call me years later when I drew latrine duty in the Air Force. The irony was not lost on me.

When the men felt like going in, or the ladies felt like coming out, all parties arose and changed venues in a well choreographed maneuver; Grandpa and Grandma passed

Clueless In Paradise

within touching distance of each other without ever exchanging word or glance. This night we kids squirreled away some salted Spanish peanuts and Orange Nesbit sodas and took refuge from the heat on our neighbors' garage roof. It was pitch black and there were stars and we felt like we were in our own world even though the folks were less than fifty feet away in the backyard. My cousins Butch and Sonny decided to drive Butch's sister, Carol, nuts but I, being the oldest and wisest, told them that if they brought attention to themselves we'd be dragged down off the roof and that would really piss me off. That seemed to work. But it was all for naught because soon after that I heard my mother call for us from down below. She said that the men were going out for a drink and wanted the boys to go along. Carol was to stay with the women. Well, we weren't going to miss this; the only time we were invited along by the men for anything was when they went hunting, and then they used us as gun bearers and retrievers. The MEN wanted us to go somewhere with them!

    We shoehorned ourselves around the men in my uncle's Chevy sedan and were off. I think the guys were already a little "happy" because the jokes and off-color remarks were flying. The best ones were in Italian; I knew they were the best by the way they laughed and because they were in Italian. If you asked what it meant you got a look that said "mind your own business". All the windows were down and the smoke from their cigarettes went blowing by. My head was out the window; I was happy as a spaniel, loving the feel of the night air on my face. Sonny hung out the opposite side while Butch was stuck between his father and another uncle; a victim of social Darwinism before there was a name for such a thing.

Sam Culotta

Where we going?
To a bar. (laughter)
Really?
Yep.

We pulled up at a tavern whose parking lot was aglow with neon beer signs. Muffled noises came through the open door. We boys piled out and followed the men into the darkly lit joint that smelled of smoke and beer, a lot like their breaths. My father and uncles bellied up to the bar and ordered beers for themselves and soft drinks and peanuts for us then gave us some coins and pointed us toward the pinball and skeeball machines. The owner didn't care if we were in there as long as we didn't hang out at the bar. But we did bother the men once in a while to give us a pickled egg or more shell peanuts. Dad munched some kind of pickled fish.

Want some of this Sam?

No thanks, Dad. (At first I didn't know who he was talking to.)

C'mon... it's good. You'll like it

They were small and headless and looked too much like the fish they were.

No thanks, Dad.

Suit yourself... you don't know what you're missing. Which is how he ended every rejected offer of food or drink. Too soon, we were back in the car heading home, windows open, smoke blowing, laughter, Italian wisecracks.

    This was amazing to us because our fathers were hard-working men, blue-collar laborers and they didn't spend time taking us to ballgames or teaching us to ice skate or do the other things fathers of a later generation would do with gusto. Sometimes it was best to not draw attention to yourself because the attention might not be what you hoped for. Our fathers did not see their role as being a source of comfort or affirmation; they didn't take us to our softball games or spend time helping with our homework. They taught us how to hunt, they told us we shouldn't let kids push us around, they told us what was expected of us when we were in the presence of our elders and about our responsibilities to bring honor to the family. And they were the enforcers when our mothers ran out of patience with us or when we crossed a line that required special treatment.

    The worst offense was insubordination, followed closely by embarrassing them in front of others, which amounted to the same thing. When your father was not around, an uncle, aunt or grandparent would suffice as *in loco parentis.* At least fifty years later on a visit to my home town, we went to a nursing facility to visit my elderly and somewhat demented Uncle Bart. At one point, he fixed me with his eyes and a chilly smile, and said he remembered how I pulled a rug out from under his son, Richard, and caused him to fall but my father didn't punish me because I faked innocence. "But I remember what you did." His chuckle sounded like ice cubes falling into a glass. (Dementia sufferers lose short term memory but seem to hold on to vivid memories from the past.) If he could have, I'm pretty sure he would have climbed out of that wheelchair and smacked me a good one up alongside my head. I admitted I remembered the incident.

I was a sneaky little bugger in those days.

When we returned home, the women announced that the coffee was on; they called it "coffee and" the "and" was anything from Italian cookies to dessert items my mother called "coogans". (To the best of my knowledge, coogan is a slang derivation of German kuchen or Jewish kugel, both are on the order of what we now call a "Danish".) This was usually the closing ceremony; once we were finished and the ladies had cleaned up the kitchen, the families began to say their goodbyes. Then they were gone,
  I was sent to bed from where I could hear a summary of the evening's events. Who did or didn't do what. Who doesn't know how to control their kids Who always manages to forget to bring something but still manages to eat like a pig. The usual stuff people say about the people they love most. In retrospect, I'm sure it was exhausting for my mother because even though there would be a few invitations to get together at one of the other relatives' houses, she knew she'd be faced with the same thing most of the thirteen nights of my grandfather's stay.
  The two weeks passed quickly and it was time to take Grandpa back to the train station. Before we left home, he gave me a silver dollar, something he sometimes did. I have a few in a drawer somewhere and will probably pass them along to my grandchildren some day.
  Once again, I lugged the multi-colored suitcase into the station filled with all its exotic sounds and smells. While the adults sat and chatted, I strolled off a little ways. There was a barber shop, a shoeshine stand and "Negro" porters in neat, colorful uniforms pushing trolley's full of luggage.

Clueless In Paradise

I made eye contact with one of them and he gave me a big smile which I returned. As a boy, I saw black people only in their assigned environments, so contact was minimal. As a little boy I once embarrassed my mother by asking a black man who was shingling our house if he spent too much time in the sun. He got a big kick out it but my mother was mortified and apologized for me anyway. She cautioned me later about saying things like that, but she couldn't really get mad because it was mostly her fault for warning me every summer to not spend too much time in the sun. I had a dark complexion and turned very brown. "You'll turn black as a negro if you do", she would say.

When the public address announcer called Grandpa's train number, we arose and walked him to his carriage. The delicious smell of travel was powerful here alongside the huge machine with its gigantic wheels and its steamy breath. When he was safely boarded we waited until the train began to move, then we waved, he waved, and the string of railroad cars rolled slowly by.

"OK, let's go", Dad said. "Tomorrow's a work day and six A.M. comes early dammit."
"Your father wears me out, Jim", was my mother's only reply.

I fondled the silver dollar in my pocket.

Blue Collar Limousine

I was introduced to the world of blue-collar working men when I was fifteen years old. Summer vacation had begun and my father said I should have a job. " I talked to Paul today and he said if you want to work this summer he'll give you a job.""
 "I'll be going to work with you?", I asked
"Yes."
"Great. OK"
"Well, it's not that easy. I want you to call Paul tonight and ask him for the job."
"But you said he said I could have the job", I pointed out.
"I want you to call him and ask for it."

I called and spoke to Paul and asked if I could come to work at his company for the summer. He said I could.

     My father got up at 5:00 AM. He didn't make me get up until 5:15. When he got up he turned on the hall light and made sure I was awake. I lay there watching the clock, my misery increasing with every click of the second hand. We were out the door by 5:45 AM and at the youngest brother's house around 6:00 A.M.. Andy was not only the youngest, he was also the slowest. Then we picked up Frank then Hal, saving Gabe, the CEO, for last. My father was foreman at an auto parts rebuilding company owned by three brothers. It was in Los Angeles, over twenty miles from our house in the

Clueless In Paradise

San Gabriel Valley.

There were no carpool lanes and there was only one east/west freeway. Traffic was hellacious, so the bosses came up with a solution: they bought a used Cadillac limousine and offered my father the opportunity to pick up them and their two non-owner brothers every morning and drive them to the shop. The upside was that Dad didn't have to use his own car and burn his own gas; the downside was he had to leave over a half hour earlier to collect the five of them from their homes and get home a half hour later after dropping them off on the way home. The old limo was parked in front of our house over the weekend.

On the first day I joined my father, I was initiated into his world. The moment the first brother got in and sat down, Dad's demeanor changed. He was always prone to profanity but I did not realize how much he was holding back for the sake of his family. Now his language turned deep blue; I had been using the "f" word for a while but I never heard it quite this way. They managed to use it in a number of parts of speech: verb, adverb, adjective, and gerund, to name a few. They used it to express hate, joy, frustration, surprise, consternation, you name it. Years later I found that same remarkable creativity in the Air Force.

They all smoked. My father and Andy smoked cigarettes but the others smoked cigars, big fat expensive cigars. To make matters worse, the bosses were cold averse and unless the weather was hot kept all the windows closed. Six in the morning, heater on, windows cranked up... a miasma of what we now call second-hand smoke. I have no idea how many years of healthy lung function I forfeited during the three summers and three Christmas vacations I worked for them.

Sam Culotta

The drive was an adventure. I was used to my father's driving; he drove assertively and aggressively and he had no patience for drivers who impeded his progress. But now he was driving his bosses to work in a long Caddie while they carried on their raucous conversations. Dad liked to veer off into the lanes reserved for cars coming on to the freeway, blow by the line of almost stationary traffic and then, at the last possible moment, cut in front of some poor guy who had hesitated for a second. He repeated this maneuver every chance he got. He wasn't afraid of tickets because their company supplied a number of traffic cops with free carburetors, fuel pumps and distributers and they in turn kept him and the bosses supplied with "courtesy cards". These were the times when traffic cops honored the courtesy card of other officers with the understanding theirs would be so honored.

After a week or so the novelty wore off and I managed to sleep most of the way in. Like most automotive related blue collar types of that time the workers were a diverse collection of earthy guys, some more coarse than others, but all colorful. The first thing I saw was a group of them hanging out in front of the door waiting for us to arrive and open up. The few moments it took to get in provided time for some wise cracks and good natured ragging which the brothers partook of with gusto.

When I walked into the shop I was hit with the aroma my father had carried home with him throughout my young life, the aroma of grease, oil and solvent. I was clearly in his world now. I followed him to his bench, the foreman's bench, where he worked on the most complex four-barrel carburetors. He held the shop record for most rebuilts in a day not just at this bench but at every bench he worked at before being promoted.

Clueless In Paradise

He was a genius at this kind of thing and I was damn proud of him. I was assigned to a back bench working with Dave an older guy who rebuilt relatively simple two barrel carbs. (Experienced men called them "carbs".) My humble responsibilities were supportive in nature: sorting and lining parts up for Dave to assemble. In a few weeks I was experienced enough to take a greater role in their assembly. (Dave also introduced me to Edmund Wilson's "Memoirs of Hecate County", a book of both literary and erotic fame. But that was education of a different kind.)

    Later that first morning, my father walked me around and introduced me to the men in the fuel pump and distributor sections. There were metal lathes and core drills, the smells of hot oil and burning metal. Curled silver shavings collected on the floor. The bases of fuel pumps were pressed against grinders producing a high whine and sparkling showers. Power screwdrivers with their spring-like cord protectors whirred then growled then grunted with satisfaction when the screw was fully seated.

    Around mid-morning I noticed a few of the men putting down their tools as though they were going home, but they were just preparing for the canteen truck's musical horn. It was break time and they were stealing an extra minute or two, not without drawing some flak from Gabe or his brother Frank who always seemed to be right there. I learned to love this time. I'd never eaten canteen truck fare and since I was earning my own money now I could buy a sweet roll or a doughnut and coffee. The same truck returned for lunch, a time for eating and griping. One day I saw Frank and a wise guy from the dirty break-down section get into a back and forth that began as good natured ribbing and ended with Frank firing him on the spot. The others looked on in amazement.

Sam Culotta

By the next day the guy was back to work and no more was said about it.

The days went by quickly my first couple of weeks, then the tedium set in and I knew what it was to have a real job. Dave and one or two others had a habit of visiting the bathroom about five minutes before the closing whistle. If one of the bosses caught them they heard about it. "Hey, if you have to pee, do it on your own damn time." It was a joke, sort of. A few others might begin washing their hands and arms over the long sink with four faucets. The soap was coarse as sand but managed to cut through most of the grease. (Now I knew why my father's fingernails were black all week long until his Saturday night bath.)

The drive home was just as slow as the morning drive, maybe worse. The mood was usually better. We went through the same routine, dropped off each brother before we could go home where Mom had dinner about ready.

"Well, here are my two hardworking men, home from work." she said, smiling at me in particular.
"How'd he do, Jim?"
"He did good"

Years later my father was still in touch with Hal, the last remaining brother. He visited him a couple of times a year. By now, I was well into my banking career which pleased Dad no end; he always hoped I would get a "white collar job" and avoid doing what he had to do to make a living. When he was no longer driving, I took him to see his old boss. When we arrived, Hal was sitting in his garage with the radio on. He was smoking his cigar. They talked about the old days, who was alive, who was sick, who had died. The language was as salty as ever.

Before we left, Al would give my father a bottle of some kind of liquor, whatever he happened to have around, and Dad would go home a happy man. I was never sure what he enjoyed more, seeing Hal or getting the liquor.

A Movin' And A Groovin'

Our family had a plum and white '57 Rambler V/8. That's right, plum and white. I know this because Dad announced it with great pride. Can you imagine a car color called plum these days? It was a purple/maroonish hue set off nicely by the white. Today it might be described in the brochure as something like "Tawny Sky". Jerry's father had a '48 or '49 deep green Oldsmobile with a straight "8" engine. Small aircraft could land on this baby. When you sat in the front seat the hood ornament looked like it was out there flying on its own ahead of the car. Our Rambler was what then was considered a sporty sedan, rounded corners and at least a couple of feet shorter than the Olds. Its engine may have had less horse power but due to its "diminutive" figure it was a match for the old powerhouse Olds.

    We had to know which was the faster car, so we went down to a stretch of road that was usually quiet at night, and set up side by side. Jerry sat there with that all business jutting jaw look of his which made me smile despite the gravity of the moment. The street was empty except for our two cars so we knew we had a good long, unimpeded stretch in which to let it all out. Jerry nodded, and we hit it.

We met early in our freshman year. I was sitting on the school lawn waiting for my bus to arrive. He was sitting alone, legs

Clueless In Paradise

akimbo, perfectly combed hair and impressive sideburns. Something about him told me he was a newcomer to the area. I probably recognized that in him since I myself had moved here with my family from Rochester, New York, only a year and a half earlier. Newcomers have a look about them. They aren't accompanied by friends and are often dressed and groomed just differently enough from the rest of us to stand out. But more than that, there is tentativeness in the way they interact with others. I sat near him and struck up a conversation. Turns out his family had moved here from Madison, Wisconsin, just a few months ago. His father was a truck driver. I told him about my recent arrival from New York and in a matter of minutes we were friends. I liked his feisty, unapologetic attitude and his working class family background.

    His family were German, mine Italian: nothing compatible there. He grew up playing basketball with his older brother, who was his hero; I grew up playing baseball with my friends and my uncle, who was my hero. Before long, he and I were inseparable. His mom worked while mine did not, so we often stopped at his house on the way home from school. She might leave a freshly baked pan of white cake, still warm when we got there. Jerry would pour us glasses of icy-cold milk and we would cut into the cake. She also made the best damned roast beef sandwiches I'd ever eaten. The meat was cut like a butcher did it, the bread was soft and white and slathered with mayonnaise. My sandwiches were often on Italian bread and filled with fried bell peppers or even (gasp) fried eggplant. (My mother learned to make sandwiches from darn near anything during the Great Depression.) The problem was, the oil in them soaked into the bread and made them really ugly. Jerry's roast beef sandwiches were perfect and cut diagonally. The cut made one side as clean a triangle as you will ever see, while the other included the rounded top which made it larger for some reason. Jerry referred to this as the "mother" half. My sandwiches were always cut in half either widthwise or vertical. If vertical they had two mother halves. Human nature being perverse, Jerry took a liking to my oily sandwiches. I was embarrassed by the gruesome looking things and lusted after his sculpted beef sandwiches. So, we often switched. On days when one of us came to school with money to buy something from the canteen, the one with the money would buy a hamburger or tamales and we would split them as well as the sandwich the other brought from home. Sometimes we vied for the "mother" half.

Jerry's father, true to his German heritage, made home-brew beer. It was rich and flavorful and possessed of more alcohol than the watered down product sold in the liquor stores. Sometimes when we were doing our homework together, his dad would let us have one apiece and it was enough to give us a nice buzz. "Man, if we could drink more of this we'd really get lit up wouldn't we?" I suggested. "Yeah," he said, "we'd really get loaded."

Our chance came one night when his parents planned a Saturday night outing and invited me to stay with Jerry while he babysat his younger brother and sister. The plan was for me to spend the night, so we would have all the time and opportunity we needed to down a few. Long story short, we drank three or four apiece and never felt a thing. To compensate, we tried to convince one another that we were drunk by wobbling around and acting stupid. To this day I don't understand why that much beer didn't get us drunk.

I was raised on baseball and some football but where Jerry came from basketball was king. He introduced me to the game and although I was a shrimp I took to it. Soon he and I were a smooth operating machine; he was a good ball handler and loved to make clever passes while I had a good shot and was quick enough to get open. He played guard and I played forward. I was a four foot eleven and he was a five foot one but on the playground we were hell on wheels. Eventually, I felt confident enough to go out for our high school basketball team with Jerry. We were put on the "D" squad, what you would now call the freshman team.

Things went reasonably well for a while, but eventually we were pushed off the starting lineup. Soon after we started the next season on the "C" team, Jerry broke his collar bone riding a horse at the stables where he worked for his uncle. All he could do from then on was help out as equipment manager. Then, I went bad. For whatever reason, I began acting out, cutting classes and eventually was suspended from school. My basketball coach agreed to give me a "D" if I would attend all the remaining practice sessions. To this day I may be the only alumnus of that school who got a "D" in basketball after having made the team.

By the following year we had both gotten our driver's licenses. We didn't have cars but Jerry wouldn't let that stop him. More than once, he snuck his father's behemoth of a car out of the garage and came to my house to get me. Of course, my parents were none the wiser; they figured he had permission to be out with the family car. Actually, I often didn't know myself until we headed out. Then he would tell me how he had rolled the big Olds down into the street and a little down the block before starting it up. A car, a bottle of Ripple wine, and we were in business. Somehow, he never got caught and we never got arrested, or killed.

My record of driving firsts is not a good one. The day I

passed my driver's license test I convinced my mother to let me borrow the family car for a short ride to visit friends. It was a 1954 Nash Statesman, four door sedan, large enough to fill a two car garage. This was the famous Nash with the fold back front seats that earned it the nickname, "the bedroom on wheels". I later used it on a few drive-in theater dates, but this occasion was far less enjoyable. Within a mile of leaving the house, I spied a couple of girls I knew walking beside the road and pulled over to say hello and announce my newly achieved status as a licensed driver. I almost swerved into the trees that bordered the road but managed to come to a safe stop. They, of course, overwhelmed by my new status, jumped into the front seat and off we went. They said they were going to a third girl's house and asked if I'd take them there. That girl decided to join us in our travels and jumped in, also in the front seat. As I said, the Nash was huge, but four of us in the front left little room to maneuver. My plan was to drop all three girls off at the house of a fourth girl, then return home.

  The driveway at the house was unpaved and rutted from a recent rain. As I navigated the behemoth into its turn, it rocked in the ruts and threw the three nubile ladies up against my right arm. With my arm now pinned, I couldn't turn the steering wheel and careened into the chain-link fence gate. The car's momentum carried us along for a yard or two before I was able to stop.

  No misery compares to the one I felt while awaiting my father's return home from work. I had shown my mother the damage: a four or five foot long gouge along the sleek side of his almost new Nash Statesman. Mom was appalled but restrained herself out of pity. She didn't have the heart to add to what was coming from my father. For the record, my father was a great guy but also a disciplinarian. He was a car man to

Clueless In Paradise

the bone and the Nash was his current pride and joy. (He would soon have the Rambler mentioned above.)

Dad got home and Mom headed him off in the driveway while I waited in the garage with the wounded whale. I don't know what she said, how she said it, or what she promised him. He raised the garage door and proceeded to walk slowly up and down assessing the damage, tossing me the occasional glance from beneath his hooded eyes. I must have looked like a puppy who had just crapped on the new sofa. Finished with his appraisal, he turned to me and, *mirabile dictu,* said in a controlled, humane tone of voice. "What happened?" I explained as best I could; I blamed the girls and the rutted driveway as much as possible. He listened. "What the hell were you thinking? Do you realize what a stupid move that was?" Yes, I surely did. Then he turned and went into the house. After dinner, we drove to my friend's and Dad offered to pay for the fence, an offer they graciously accepted.

About a year later my father brought home a black, six cylinder, 1946 Chevy coupe. He said a man he worked with was getting rid of it and would sell it cheap. He wanted me to drive it and see if I liked it. Cheese and crackers!!! Like it? I would have liked a lawn mower with a seat! This was to be my car, my very own car! If I remember correctly, he got it for two hundred dollars. The deal was that he bought it but I was responsible for gas, general maintenance and insurance. What a deal. I guess memories of what I had done to his Nash had faded. I told you he was a good guy at heart. We took a get-acquainted drive so he could be sure I was able to handle the column stick shift and learn the controls. The transmission had what they called a vacuum shift. When you changed gears you could feel and hear it go into the next gear with a slight whoosh. I realized immediately it would not do well in a drag race, but that's another story.

As soon as I could get away from the dinner table I called Jerry and announced my good fortune and said I was on my way over to show him the car. By the time I picked him up, it was dark but that didn't make much difference, I mean, the car was black and shined in the street lamps so what more could you ask for? He climbed in and we headed out all excited and feeling like newly sprung convicts. It had begun to rain just a little bit so we both fumbled around with the controls until we found a small plastic knob that activated the windshield wipers. The wipers also ran on vacuum so they went whoosh, whoosh, while the gear shift went whoosh, and the visibility got worse.

I drove down one of the major avenues toward a café we liked and as I approached a four way intersection Jerry threw his arm against my chest and shouted for me to stop. I did. I was about to ask him what the hell he was doing when I heard the sirens and saw a white Ford T-Bird careen through the intersection go into a sideways slide and hit the curb on the far side of the street. The T-Bird flipped, the doors flew open and two bodies flopped out onto the asphalt parking lot of a super market. Right behind the T-Bird came a police unit, siren screaming, wheels screeching. As we watched in amazement the bodies that had flown out of the T- Bird jumped up off the ground and ran like hell, followed by the police in hot pursuit. Jerry and I looked at each other and said "Shit!" at the same time. I proceeded through the intersection then took Jerry home and went home myself. That was enough excitement for my Chevy for one night.

We graduated together. The process was in alphabetical order so Jerry went before me followed a short while later

Clueless In Paradise

by our friend Barbara whose fence I took down with the Nash. Until now, each graduate was greeted with a round of polite applause and sometimes a whistle or two. Then, they called my name. My father was not one to miss an opportunity to rejoice, or to embarrass his son. As I processed forward his voice came booming out of the stands: "way to go, Culotta!" I heard some chuckles and imagined my mother jabbing him in the ribs. But, I wasn't embarrassed at all.

I have a photo of Jerry and me just after the ceremony, my sharkskin gray suit is reflecting the light, Jerry looks dapper and leans in towards me. His hair looks better than mine because when I'm shorn, as I was there, I'm all ears. We are holding our diplomas with pride. Later that night we went to the Senior Party held in a rented hall somewhere. Jerry had gotten hold of a pint of Peppermint Schnapps and a bottle of Four Roses whiskey. He was driving but we managed to suck down the Schnapps on the way to the hall. A while later when we were well into the Four Roses I got sick, something I excelled at throughout my youth and early adulthood. I don't remember how Jerry held up but he had a stronger stomach than I did so he probably avoided my fate. When I returned to the dance party I learned that I had won a drawing for a 45 rpm record of Bobby Darin's "Splish Splash". What luck!

Splish splash I was taking a bath
Long about a Saturday night..
Rub dub just relaxing in the tub
Thinking everything was alright.

Sam Culotta

We got back to my house just as my father was coming out the door on his way to work. He was amused by evidence of our wild night. I told Mom we were going to change clothes and head over to a nearby friend's where a few of us alumni were gathering. "You two aren't going anywhere until you lie down and sleep for a few hours" I started to protest but realized, graduates or not, she was still the boss. Later, after a nap, we did go.

Jerry and I enrolled at a local community college but it didn't work out. He got a job driving truck and I eventually dropped out because I was in love with my wife-to-be and couldn't concentrate. He went into the Army; I went into the Air Force. He embarked on a "serious" relationship, and I became engaged. Later, when we were both back home and married with children, we got together a few times. Then he moved with his family upstate to dairy country and settled down to drive a milk truck. I began a financial services career that carried me to retirement.

We exchanged a few letters and annual Christmas cards and then the contact ended all together. As our Fiftieth class reunion approached, I became involved with the alumni and tried to track him down. A friend gave me his number and I called. It was a strange conversation because it had been so long since we'd been in touch, and he was so hard of hearing I had to shout. Eventually, he turned the phone over to his wife who said they would make an effort to come down. They didn't, and that was that.

> *Well, I stepped out the tub*
> *put my feet on the floor*
> *I wrapped a towel around me*
> *And I opened the door*

Clueless In Paradise

    We pushed the pedals to the metal, as they say. One of us, I don't know who, burnt a little rubber and off we went. I glanced over at Jerry once more to see him slam the Olds into second gear. The Rambler had an automatic transmission so it just stayed in passing gear until it leveled out in high gear. We were jockeying back and forth, our headlight beams danced out in front of us, leading the way down the dark asphalt road....

and with a splish, splash
I jumped back in the bath,
how was I to know there was a party going on.

Mangiare Di Tutto *

I don't care much for honey. I don't dislike it; I like it a bit when it is incorporated into other comestibles, like cough drops or baked goods, but I don't care for it one on one. I know people who enjoy spooning it out and dribbling it onto their tongues. One person I know can consume a jar of it in one sitting. Mine is not a particularly unusual disaffection. My wife has no love for pancakes, watermelon, corn-on-the-cob, iced tea and juices of all kinds, which seems to me more unusual. I know people who don't like nuts in baked goods or chocolate, others who cannot enjoy pasta unless it is in the form of spaghetti. This one astounds me. I mean, take a string of spaghetti, flatten it out into linguini and they won't eat it. To me, raised on pasta in all its heavenly variety, this seems insane. My father, a second generation Sicilian, was one of these. When my mother made any other shape for company she had to make a pot of spaghetti for her husband. I did have a slight aversion to lasagna when I was a boy. Thankfully, I overcame that problem and enjoy it immensely now.

    Pasta, or as we called it before the "enlightenment", macaroni, was an indispensible part of my childhood. The smell from a pot of simmering sauce sets off my taste buds and brings tears to my eyes. Sauce needs to cook for hours to reach its peak of flavor; this is part of its considerable charm. On many a Sunday we went to my grandparents' house for dinner. From the moment we walked in the door until we ate

Clueless In Paradise

hours later the aroma of the simmering sauce was everywhere. It was in the air we breathed. We kids were sometimes allowed to dip a chunk of Italian bread into the pot but woe unto those who dipped without permission. Grandma and her wooden spoon were never far away. When we didn't go to Grandma's, Mom put the Sunday pot on at home so when we returned from Mass the first thing to assault our senses was that heavenly same aroma. Our Zenith radio, (ivory colored plastic with a patina of nicotine), pumped out "The Italian Hour" to magnify the effect.

Sicilians love seafood. I guess it's because they come from an island where fishing is the primary industry and means of survival. This makes the fact that fish played a minor role in my family's diet unusual. The main culprit was, once again, my father. Being Catholic, we had fish most Fridays but it took the form of what was called "fish fry" in those days. Basically, you take some sort of white fish like cod and drop it in boiling oil. On rare occasions we went out for fish-fry at a restaurant where it was served with French-fried potatoes. This and tuna fish were about all we ate when we couldn't have meat. (I read a novel written by a Sicilian writer recently and was gagged by all the octopus and sea urchin the protagonist ate.)

My people also enjoy lamb a lot, but to get it by my father's otherwise dysfunctional nose my mother had to cook it early and dress it up like beef. I was with dad on this one. A lamb chop I could enjoy but mutton was disgusting. I recall my father taking a few bites then putting down the fork and looking at my mother with suspicion. "What is this?" he'd ask. "Beef", she'd answer. "Are you sure? Smells like damn mutton to me." She'd try to deny it again but knew the jig was up.

A nice little back and forth would ensue during which my father expressed his sense of betrayal and my mother countered by blaming the tight food budget he allowed her. Fact is, she really liked lamb and just thought it would be nice to have some once in a while.

    Meal times were often the scene of colorful family interaction. Add in a mother-in-law or father-in-law, a couple of aunts and uncles and you had a sociological Petri dish. Later when I was in Air Force boot camp I found the same dynamic existed. Of all the miserable things we had to take part in, the event most fraught with danger was the visit to the chow hall. I liken it to the watering hole where the poor gazelles are forced to go for sustenance knowing lions lurked there.

    In the chow hall as at the dinner table you are confined to intimate surroundings with no easy means of escape. The lions in the case of the chow hall are the TI's, or Training Instructors, many of them aspiring or accomplished sadists. We were at their mercy as we lined up to have the food-stuff plopped on our trays. We marched through the line sideways, at attention and were allowed to speak only in response to questions from the food Nazi's behind the counter. "What the hell you want?" "Some more potatoes, please?" "Gave you goddam potatoes...move it!" To make matters worse, we knew the TI's were laying bets as to whose troops would perform better. If you screwed up and cost your sergeant his bet there was hell to pay.

    My people were much nicer but no less vigilant. Everyone at the table whether young or old, immediate family or "amici" was under Mom's clandestine observation. "No more?...you're not hungry today? You don't like the meatballs? I know there are pigs' feet...you always eat the meatballs even when you eat the pigs' feet. You probably filled up on the bread didn't you?

Clueless In Paradise

That's why I never put bread out when we have macaroni. Why do you need more starch? Look at me, I've had ten ravioli; they're delicious this time even if I say so myself. Adeline, eat more! All you do is pick at your salad. I've never seen anyone eat so slow, it's no wonder your husband takes the food off your plate! My son eats as much as I do, don't you honey. He loves ravioli as much as I do. I've got more in the kitchen so ask if you want more. Her favorite statement of frustration and/or disgust was: "You're turning my food to poison!" delivered with great volume and dramatic emphasis.

After a gargantuan feast the men left the table and the ladies cleaned up. In just a short while the table would be reset with coffee cups and dessert plates. If it was a special occasion there might be cannoli and Italian cookies. Italian cookies are completely different than most other cookies, certainly not like American ones. They are not heavily sweetened; they derive their delicate flavor from touches of liqueur and sometime, herbs. Instead of a sudden rush of sweetness there is a subtle building of flavor that reaches its pinnacle just as you swallow and take a sip of coffee or milk. This leaves you longing for the next bite. Needless to say, many non-Italians are disappointed when they first try them. Some, like my brother-in-law, never eat them again. He, by the way, is the same person who can slurp down an entire jar of honey. Go figure.

I don't remember anyone not liking cannoli although my father always complained they didn't taste like the one's he had "back east", meaning Rochester, N.Y. "They make the damn things with ricotta out here. They never made them back east with ricotta, they made them with custard." When my mother managed to find them made with the custard filling he complained that the custard didn't taste like the one back east.

Years later when my wife and I visited Rochester, we made a special effort to go to the Italian bakery section of town and purchase the iconic custard-filled cannoli with the chocolate jimmies on the end. At the next big dinner we presented them to him. "Ah, they're better, but even *they* don't make 'em the way they used to" And so it went.

I have to smile when I hear sociologists and others bemoan the fact that today's families do not sit down together to share meals. They're right, of course, but their recommendations should come with a warning:" Not all family dinners are conducive to your mental health." Then again, what's mental health in comparison to my mother's ravioli and a batch of back-east cannoli?

" Eat up! Eat it all up!"

An Accidental Education

Economics 101

Our high school had "home rooms". I'm not sure such things exist today. The idea was there should be a nesting place for the students to gather for an hour every day. We were assigned by alphabetical order to our specific home rooms. There was no instruction, only supervision, the idea being that the time should be used for study and homework. How the teachers were chosen for these rooms remains a mystery to me but our home room teacher was Miss Baylor. I don't know her age; from the perspective of a fourteen year old freshman, she seemed middle-aged and had the matronly mannerisms of what was then called, a spinster. Miss Baylor's most notable characteristic was an aversion to discipline. It took only one or two days for miscreants such as myself to realize anything short of setting the room on fire would be ignored or overlooked. Soon my cronies and I were spending all our time talking among ourselves and pestering the girls.

    My best friend and I had seats in the back of the room next to the rear door which opened out onto the grassy area between buildings, so we smoked on occasion. Miss Baylor must have known but seemed to avert her face rather than be forced to challenge us. We found ourselves pitying the much abused lady. Whether this was due to a visit from the Holy

Spirit or, more likely, the fact that it just wasn't fun anymore. Too easy.

Our home room assignment remained the same throughout the years. It got so bad at one time that some of us would ask for a hall pass to use the restroom, (which the dear lady never refused but did caution us to not take too long), leave, and never return. As it happened, when graduation day was nigh classes began ending and all that was left was finishing off small details. The small details my friend and I had to finish off were a couple of leftover demerits from our earlier misbehavior. We had to sit in a classroom with a few other students for one hour under the watchful eye of Miss Baylor. By now there was little at stake and we had long ago mended our relationship with her, so we spent the time in amiable conversation.

Back in my freshman year when Miss B. still made febrile attempts to control me, she decided one day to scold me but in the process could not come up with my name. "Now you stop your chatting back there, do you hear me? Yes, you, er, you, er.. what IS your name?" For no reason I've ever been able to recall, I answered: "George". From that day on she called me George. Now, about to be shut of me and my ilk and feeling expansive, she took advantage of our conversational moment:

"May I ask you a personal question?"

"Of course, Miss Baylor, what is it?"

"I've always wondered why you are called George when your name is listed as Sam."

"Oh," I said, "my name is Sam, of course. I just told you George that day because it was the first name that popped into my head!"

Actually, I had begun to like her in recent months and this only reinforced my feelings. She and my friend and I had a good chuckle over that. I was pleased to see she did in fact have a sense of humor.

"Now, may I ask *you* a personal question?"

"I suppose," she said, betraying a tiny bit of trepidation.

"I know you are a well educated and a well qualified person. So why on earth do you not get a job teaching at a college instead of putting up with rabble like us?" I will never forget the almost Mona Lisa smile that crossed her lips before she said:

"Because this pays way better than a college job."

La Donna e Mobile, Or, The Power of Nuns

Her name was Barbara W. and we were in the first grade. She was my first crush. In the second grade I found two stunning blonds, both named Judy. Judy M. was of German extraction while Judy K. was from a Polish family. The two Judys were the focus of my attention through to the fourth grade when they were supplanted by Pat M., either of German or Irish extraction, I never knew, or cared. For a brief time in the seventh grade I wooed Sheila, a dark-haired beauty of unknown origin. In retrospect I wonder at there being a Sheila in our all Catholic school populated mostly by the children of German families. (Ours was one of only two Italian families in the entire parish.) I don't think there is a St. Sheila. Be that as it may, I asked her to the movies and she accepted, becoming my first official date.

The movie will be forever un-remembered because I spent the entire time "necking" with her in the dark balcony. At least I thought we were necking. It amounted to my arm around her shoulder and our heads tilted together. The result of an hour or so of this was a painful cramp in my arm and a sore neck that I nursed the rest of that weekend. I'm certain the experience was just as uncomfortable for her. When we stepped out of the theater her mother was waiting for her. We said goodbye, she went to her mother and I, somewhat relieved, turned on my heel and walked home in the gloaming.

The following Monday we met at school and hung around together at recess as couples were wont to do in those days. A few days later she turned cold on me, wouldn't walk with me, barely spoke and stayed with her girlfriends. I was not all that experienced in the field of romance but I sensed something had changed, so when I got the chance I asked one of her friends what was the matter with Sheila. She told me that Sheila had experienced a change of heart; she had decided to become a nun. Imagine my chagrin: one date with me and she chose to deny her burgeoning young lady-hood and take the cloth, dedicate herself to Christ, take a vow of chastity. I accept the fact that I wasn't a great "necker" but I can't believe I drove her into a cloistered life. Girls!

Consumer Lending

Anyone who has served in the military knows that the principal means of survival involves lending, or as it's also referred to, bumming. You're being marched around by the drill sergeant and he decides to grant a five minute rest period. You come to a precision (you hope) halt, he orders "right face!" Then he commands: "Pah rade... rest!" After a pregnant pause he adds the words you've been praying to hear: "At ease! Smoke'm if you gott'em." Thank God, you sigh. But when we troops reach into our pockets for cigarettes, a certain number of us were sure to come up empty.

"Oh, shit! I left mine in the barracks. Can I bum one off you?" And so it begins. Somebody is out of smokes, somebody can't find their flashlight and most certainly, somebody needs change to get a cold drink from the vending machine when we are given brief area liberty. After a few weeks, no one remembers who owes whom what. Who cares. All you want to do is survive basic training.

Once you arrive at your first permanent assignment things take a turn for the better. At first you all live in the barracks. Eventually, some get married or are joined by their wives, and are allowed to live in off-base housing. Most continue to live in the barracks. Now the greatest need is not smokes but folding cash. A percentage of guys are guaranteed to blow through their pay before the next payday arrives and the inter-squad financial activities begin. I can attest to this because after I bought my fiancé a beautiful engagement ring on credit I became a borrower. The payments cost me almost fifty percent of my monthly income. In no time at all I became a leech.

I made the ring payment with the first of my bi-monthly checks, which left me with ten dollars or so to make it to the next payday. When my money ran out I began borrowing judiciously. On my next payday I repaid my debts, which left me sort of cash strapped again... and so forth. I never failed to repay my debtors the moment I got paid so my credit standing with the jewelry store and with my pals, was terrific. It's how I was raised; missing a ring payment or not repaying my buddies was unthinkable. Meet Will Bunker.

Willie, as we called him, was a large, slow moving man. A career enlisted man with little chance of retiring as a sergeant. His uniform, which was always crisply starched with razor sharp creases, seemed stressed to the limit to contain his massive arms and thighs. He was generally amiable as indicated by the slight smile that adorned his jowls. Thankfully, he and I became friends of a sort, meaning I felt safe in his presence.

One night when we were on shift together we got to talking about life, as guys in uniform are wont to do. We discussed the intricacies of lending and borrowing money. He revealed he was in debt to a couple of guys for a sizable chunk of money."Damn, Willie. That would drive me nuts knowing I owed that much money. Doesn't it bother you?" "Nah", said Willie with that smile which now looked more like a sneer, "I figure the guy who has to get the money back is the one that should worry, not me."

Ecce Homo

I attended St. Michael's grammar school through the seventh grade. We were taught by the Sisters of Notre Dame, a particularly strict order headquartered in Boston, MA.

Clueless In Paradise

Corporal punishment was not unusual, nor was intimidation and downright brain washing, but it was all done for the best of reasons: to inculcate into young minds a system of religious belief and an ethos of respectable behavior. Over the course of time these nuns, and the priests who made occasional visits to the classroom, took on an aura of sanctity, of otherworldliness. We might chafe under their rule but would never see ourselves as equals in the eyes of the Lord.

We moved to California from New York during the summer between my seventh and eighth grades. My parents would have liked me to continue my parochial school education, (it was markedly better than a public school education at the time), but finances and distance to the school made them susceptible to my petitions to go public. But under the close scrutiny of my parents, I continued in my faithful adherence to the Church.

It wasn't easy. I was a teenager now, subject to all the pitfalls of that turbulent phase of life. Like rising ocean currents, hormones coursed through my body in waves that crashed against the bulwark of my fast deteriorating resolve. I became surly, cocky and often rebellious. In no time I was getting into trouble at school and engaging in anti-social behavior, nothing terrible, but not in keeping with the ethos hammered into me by the nuns and my parents. But I did continue to practice my religion, practice being the operative term. My new lifestyle resulted in the need to see a confessor regularly.

Over time I established a pattern of behavior that brought me to the attention on one particular priest. Father Bowman was a young, good natured, priest who prided himself on an ability to "relate" to teens such as myself. I would see him around the church from time to time and we began to talk about things... worldly things..nothing religious, more like pals. Father even asked me once to run an errand for him to pick up an awning he had purchase but was unable to fetch. I fulfilled the assignment and even found pleasure in being helpful. The idea of earning points with God may have been considered. All in all, I was fine with the arrangement but was leery of getting too involved with a "man of the cloth". Confession is the bane of any Catholic boy's existence. The only saving grace was an assurance that whatever was confessed or discussed in that dark closet with its faint aroma of incense would be kept in complete secrecy, "retained" by the priest. The curtain or shield between you provided privacy; this was between you, the priest and God... no one else.

    Not long after delivering the awning to Father, I had occasion to visit the confessional. Things went along as well as could be expected: there was the usual revelation of bad behavior, the ensuing guidance and/or corrective instructions, issuance of my penance and my Act of Contrition. I left the confessional with a sense of relief and every intention to do better in the future.

    Deep in my heart I knew I'd be back in a week or so. But for now, I was a happy soul and proceeded to find a quiet pew in which to say my Hail Mary and Our Fathers as sentenced. The door to the confessional opened and out stepped Father Bowman. I ducked my head hoping he wouldn't notice me. I would be embarrassed to know he knew who had just unburdened his soul to him. He came over to me and in a quiet voice I was sure resounded throughout the church and thanked me for running the errand for him. The other penitents stopped their prayers for a moment out of curiosity, then returned to their whispering. Father returned to the confessional. I slithered out the pew and left.

Yearbook Therapy

Feeling bad? Life got you down? Career going nowhere? Relationships stale? You bent down to pet your dog and it snarled? The decades piling up like dandruff on your collar? I know the feeling. Everyone over a certain age experiences this let down. Some call it a mid-life crisis but we can get it in our thirties just as easily as in our forties, or fifties, or later. You can talk to your doctor and she or he will be more than happy to prescribe an anti-depressant medication. Oh, yes. At the slightest hint of depression out comes the questionnaire:

Constant feeling of sadness, anxiety, emptiness?
General sense of pessimism?
Feeling of hopelessness?
Feeling restless?
Experiencing irritability?
Have you lost interest in activities or hobbies you once enjoyed?
Lost interest in sex?
Find it hard to concentrate, remember details, make decisions?
Low level of energy, feeling fatigue?
Sleep patterns disturbed?
Eating habits changed: eating too much, or have no appetite?
Suicidal thoughts?
Aches and pains, cramps, headaches or digestive problems?

If you didn't answer yes to more than a couple of these you are either a medical and psychological marvel or a liar. (I could have answered yes to three or four of these questions when I was in my twenties!) Of course there are many levels and types of depression; they can be debilitating or life changing, they may be only temporary, like the blues. So, if you think you may only have the blues, try this before you turn to medicine or booze: High School Yearbook.

A few days ago I had occasion to look into mine to verify that someone my sister met went to my high school. As I wandered through it I was drawn to comments my classmates had written to me during those heady days just before graduation when every senior walks around campus with their yearbook in hand ready to trade entries with anyone they recognize. Some of these are heartfelt, made with all the best intentions, others are more like the things you write when a birthday card is passed around the office.

One of my dearest friends wrote:

"We've had such a great time all four years together. I can remember when you were my latest heart throb...you didn't even know I was alive. Remember all the great "jam sessions" we had? I don't think a week-end passed when we weren't dancing or at the show.

I still think of all the fun we had at the swimming pool too. We used to dunk each other until we couldn't breathe. Most of that fun is gone now. *It seems since we've grown up and gotten to be seniors that all of our good times have gone with our younger years.*" (Italics mine.)

Clueless In Paradise

Good grief! World weary already, and she was only eighteen when she wrote this. Ironically, she was one of the most life-loving, crazy-in-a-good way people I ever knew. Just before she passed away from cancer she told me she had warned her son he had better get the cat's ashes off his mantle and make room for hers!

A more traditional entry:

" Roger, I sure have had a ball my senior year and I want to wish you lots of luck in the future. Know you enjoyed every minute of it too. {wrong}... Hope your wishes come true. You're a cool head, from a potential genius.
(P.S. just kidding about the genius bit.)"
He was an original surfer boy...drove a real Woody. A cool head, indeed.

From a girl I knew casually but never dated:

"Dear Roger, (Sam)
That's what you get for calling me Lilly.
You are a real nice guy and I want to wish you all of the success and happiness you could ever hope for. I sincerely hope to see you again. Be good and work hard to get your goal. It was really a pleasure knowing you. Your friend always until H___ freezes over and all the little devils go ice skating."

That is so sweet. She was a cool chick but I've not seen her since we graduated over fifty years ago. I'm sure she meant every word because a person's true feelings always surface at the end of high school.
How about this?:

Sam Culotta

"To My Brother
Who deserves the very best of luck in the world because your [sic] swell.
The best of luck and success through your first year of College,
Love, Sis"

    She was only ten at the time. Pretty darned good for ten, I'd say. Right up there with some of my classmates. And her wishes worked too. I have had a lot of luck and success, and some still consider me swell.

This one made me feel pretty good:

"Well handsome, it has been 1/2 a panic knowing you this year and listening to your troubles with the women of this day and age. I hope next year you will have them all quite under control - maybe even in a harem. So stop messing around_____. I wish you all the luck and happiness in the world - live it up now- after the Sr. Party you may be too tired."
                              Bye from another mighty Senior
                                            J."

Well, J, I did my best but a harem just wasn't in my future. And I really was too tired and sick to live it up after the Sr. Party. (I'd forgotten I was a 1/2 a panic. Imagine a full panic!)

 Xavier was the only person I've ever known whose name begins with an "X".

Clueless In Paradise

"It sure has been fun knowing you. I will always remember you because you helped me a lot in English. (Remember?) . Well what more or what can I wish you than the best of luck in your future."
     Your friend, X'

     Xavier may have known something; after I retired from banking I became a tutor for ESL and writing at a local college. Thanks, buddy.

     I like this one because it was written by a guy who joked about the cowboy belt buckle I wore my first day in Junior High. I had moved to California from New York state that summer and was not really hip to the scene, if you know what I mean.

"We sure had fun this year at school. It has been just great. You're a riot!   Have fun this summer and don't work too hard. See you at Sac.{Mt. San Antonio College} M."

 Well, I could go on but in truth there are only a few other entries in my year book. I wasn't what you would call "a sosh" and I wasn't comfortable going around soliciting contributions. Most of the people who wrote in my book were people who knew me and asked to write something. As a matter of fact, I realized while writing this that my very best friend, with whom I was so close we were often considered a unit, did not write in my book. To be honest, I don't know if I wrote in his either. That heartrending fact aside, you can see why reading these remarks would lift a person out of the doldrums.

Finally, here is a comment that sums up the entire experience better than any other. It was written by a young lady who became a very good friend in just the final year of school.

She writes:
"..........but one thing, I don't want you to ever forget me or I'll be broken hearted and I mean it. We all have to keep in touch and never forget each other. And I'll never forget you. Love always, J."

I was characteristically distant after graduation. In fact, it wasn't until over forty years had passed before I was contacted by a lady who had been my girlfriend for a time back then. She convinced me to attend an annual event for all graduates of our school. I did so for close to ten years and never saw "J", or "X" or "M" or my best friend. Only "P", Phyllis showed up for the picnic the day before our Fiftieth Class Reunion. Others may have been at the actual event the next evening but, alas, I didn't attend.

I hope this has been helpful. Personally, I'm depressed again.

Christmas Eve, 1961

Not only love can break a heart, an empty airport on Christmas Eve can do a pretty good job of it. The only voice you hear is the disembodied vocals of the PA system announcing departures but no arrivals. Or maybe it was the other way around. I pace across the tile floors, my military shoes echo off the walls half-heartedly. In the coffee shop there is a man wearing a rain coat, the kind detectives wear in cop movies. We drink coffee and smoke cigarettes from opposite ends of the counter. He must be a regular traveler because the waiter leans toward him as they talk just loud enough to not be heard. The coffee's not bad for airport coffee and I move the cup from place to place thinking of Eliot's poem… something about counting the days in empty cups or spoons, or coffee rings. I wish I could remember, damn it. "I have measured out my life in coffee spoons" there it is! You get a lot of time to think sitting in a coffee shop near midnight. The cigarette is beginning to taste like the smell of an overstuffed ash tray.

    I've brought a book to read but can't bear to open it up. "Too Late the Phalarope" by Alan Paton, a South African writer. It was given to me by a casual friend from my dismal college years when I was making a half-hearted effort to get a degree education on the cheap. A rare bird for the group of people I know, he's quite literate, well-read, and suffers from some sort of skeletal abnormality that gives him that artistic look we wannabe's strive to achieve. Funny thing is, he stole the book from the public library so his generosity is not without irony. He introduced me to Rabelais's Gargantua and Pantagruel, a monstrous satire with oversized organs and grotesque characters that we found really exciting. I think he and his family moved away so I probably won't see him again. I started to read the Paton book while I was on leave, but it's just not working for me. I should have brought "Catcher in the Rye"; I can read Salinger over and over. The kid in "Catcher" is the universal misfit teen, the one most of us think we are. So, maybe it's best I don't have it with me since I'm already feeling lower than whale shit.

    My plane to Spokane, WA. doesn't leave for a while yet. I've never been there but it sounds nice. What sadistic company clerk schedules a guy to report to his first permanent assignment on Christmas Day? It's a rhetorical question of course, we're talking about the military here. Speaking of which, the few people I've seen since I boarded the plane in L.A. didn't seem to care one damn bit that I'm a man in uniform, a proud Airman Third Class in the Air Force of these United States. No siree, no respect, not even a mention of my status as a protector of their freaking freedoms. In fact, the stewardess in Los Angeles had the audacity to scold me for not putting my duffle bag in the overhead compartment. Excuse me! I was a little bit distracted by the sight of my young fiancée's tear-streaked face peering over the fence.

    That same pretty face is why I bombed out in college. At least that's my excuse. Truth be told, I was wandering aimlessly around campus with no plans. But you learn things in college in spite of yourself. I learned that career counselors are about as useful as a third nostril, When I felt I had drifted so far off track as to be wasting my time, I gave counseling a try. Here is what he offered: "What do you want to be?" Really? I told him that was why I was sitting across from him; I didn't know what to do or where to go. "Finish the class you're failing now and let's see where we go from there." Turns out that where we go from there is into the Air Force. My high school counselor wasn't much better. I only saw him when I needed discipline. He once threw me out of an assembly because I was combing my hair during the National Anthem. In retrospect, it was a stupid thing to do.

"The Voice" announces an arrival. I walk over to the observation window and watch a jet land, then taxi to a resting place. I hear voices. People have appeared out of nowhere full of excitement and with arms filled with gaily wrapped Christmas gifts. In a few minutes the arrivals flow into the terminal amid much gleeful noise. There is kissing and hugging and laughter. "Merry Christmas" someone shouts. I look at my watch and I notice it's midnight, the hour my family traditionally begins opening presents. Well, this is nice, I tell myself. I'm standing here alone in the Portland airport at midnight watching complete strangers immersing themselves in the warmth of family and the joy of Christmas. At least I think I'm alone. As I take a seat and light up another cancer stick, I notice an elderly lady walking over toward me. She steps into a phone booth and drops in some coins. The happy family has departed so I can hear every word she says.

"Hi, honey, it's Mom.
No, I'm alright, really. Is he still angry?
I know, I know. I didn't mean to become a problem; I'm so sorry it upset you and the kids. Are they doing OK, now?

That's good. Please give them a big hug and kiss from Grandma, and tell them I love them so very much and I'm sorry I didn't see them before I left. What? Oh, that's OK. Yes dear, I know you love me and I'm sure your husband doesn't dislike me. It's just difficult being a mother-in-law staying with your daughter's family and not getting in the way.
     Yes, I understand. I'm sure it will all work out. I just felt it was best for me to leave and let you and your family get back to normal. I want you to know that I've purchased life insurance for the flight and I've named you and the children as beneficiaries of my estate. Now, don't be upset. I don't want you to worry, I just want you to know in case something happens. Oh, I know nothing's going to happen but just in case it does, I wanted you to be aware that I purchased the insurance. OK? Now, now, darling, please don't worry about me, I'll be just fine. I understand and I blame myself as much as anybody for what happened. Now, I'm going to have to go because I think they're about to call my flight soon.
Yes, I will… and I do love you so much.
OK, then, bye bye sweetheart, bye bye."

     As she leaves the booth she's sniffling a little. I put my head down so she doesn't know I've been listening to her conversation.
"Hello, young man. I see you're in the Air Force. Where are you stationed?"
"Spokane, I tell her"
"Oh, that's where I'm going too. We must be on the same flight."
"Yes, I suppose we are"
"Well, let's hope it's a smooth trip. Maybe I'll see you on the airplane."

Clueless In Paradise

Small and fragile looking, she walks toward the gate area. Sweet as she is, she's managed to add trepidation to the list of miseries I'm feeling. It's only the third flight of my entire life and now it may be my last. I think about insurance but I have nothing to bequeath and I'm sure the U.S. Government would have to pay some sort of benefit to my parents. That's small comfort given the circumstances.

I find my seat and stow my duffle bag in the overhead compartment to avoid getting scolded by the stewardess this time. I look around for the old lady but I don't see her. All I need is for her sit near me so we can hold hands as the plane goes down. I think I'm in the clear. It's after one A.M. and in the dim light of the coach I settle down to sleep, perchance to dream, but I know I won't. My seat is only a couple of rows behind the cockpit and stewardesses are busy in the galley or whatever that is. Occasionally, they or a crew member goes into or comes out of the cockpit and I hear the voices of the captain and crew before the door whooshes closed. One of the stewardesses is talking to them with the door held open and I hear the captain or navigator tell her that there are storms over the mountains between here and Spokane and so it's likely to be a bumpy ride. "Announce to the passengers that we may experience turbulence but that they should not be concerned as the captain will attempt to skirt most of the storm."

With that, she said something like, "Oh, great!" and let the door close. I quickly scan the seats once again in search of my melancholy dame. I don't see her, but that does nothing for my peace of mind. I remember the joke about a guy who was told he shouldn't be afraid to fly because "when it's your time, it's your time, and when it's not, it's not. No matter what the circumstances." He answers: "Yeah, but what if I'm on the same plane as someone else whose time it is?"

    I close my eyes as we accelerate down the runway. Even with the fear I feel, this is still pretty damned exciting. My very first flight was only three weeks ago when I flew home from San Antonio, Texas. That time, a really sweet stewardess noticed my nervousness and asked to hold my hand during take-off. Given the circumstances I had no choice but to be brave. But I wasn't prepared for the way it feels when the sensation of ground speed is replaced by one of floating as the plane leaves the ground. I thought we were going down and I may have squeezed her hand a bit harder. By now, I'm an old pro and I look forward to that exhilarating feeling. We leave mother earth nicely.

    I feel myself relax a bit and hope I can fall asleep soon. Maybe I can sleep through the turbulence. Thoughts of my family celebrating Christmas Eve without me, keep me awake for a while longer. It isn't as bad as we had been warned it might be. I look out the window as the plane banks and the moon is lighting up the snow on the mountains. For a few minutes I forget to be frightened; I enjoy the beauty and serenity of the scene below. Maybe the lady was wrong and took a different plane. Or maybe... Try to get some sleep, I tell myself. But everything: the flight, the prospect of my first posting, my loneliness, the image of my girlfriend crying at the gate, of my family celebrating Christmas Eve without me, keep me awake for a while longer. Then I sleep.

    I wake to the sound of electronic chimes. I'm not dead, so I must have slept a little. The captain announces we are beginning our approach into Spokane International Airport. As he says this, I feel the plane begin its descent and I hear the engines change tune. I figure, so far, so good. In a few minutes we bank to my side and I look out again at the fields of snow.

Clueless In Paradise

Pinpricks of light, probably street lights interrupt the otherwise barren looking snowscape. Before long I see that the street lights are joined by the lights of buildings and houses. I don't know why anyone would be up at this time but remember again its Christmas Eve. Now I can see what appears to be a cluster of lights in the distance which I figure are from the airport. I put my head back as we once again straighten out and continue our descent. I realize now that I've shifted my focus from where I've been to where I'm going.

The air is cold, snow is on the ground and the airport terminal is almost as empty as the one I left in Portland. My instructions are to take a taxi to the air base, a distance of ten or so miles. The sight of a woebegone looking kid in an ill-fitting Air Force dress uniform must be an everyday occurrence around here because, once again, no one pays me the slightest bit of attention as I wander around collecting my gear. Well, one guy notices me: a cab driver. "Need a ride to the base?" he asks. "Yes, sir." I'm nervous enough to call the shoe shine boy sir at this point in my military career. "Right this way, Airman" he says. That's me, the Airman, I think. The drive to the base takes about twenty minutes or so. I've never ridden in a cab, at least not when I've had to pay, so when he stops and unloads my stuff I pay him five dollars, enough to include a tip, I hope.

The Air Policeman at the gate looks at my orders and directs me toward a building about fifty yards away where I'm greeted by a couple of "old timers", Airmen 2nd class not much older than I am but with one stripe more. One of them processes my paperwork and then orders me to grab my gear and follow him to a truck.

We stop at a barracks for guys who arrive but haven't been assigned yet to their units. There is a day room with four bunks. One is occupied by a kid from Camden, New Jersey. He talks with that strong Jersey accent slightly reminiscent of the New York sound of my youth in Rochester. I don't know why, but he tells me he's Jewish, maybe to head off any talk about how sad it is to be here in the wee hours of Christmas morning. He has his own problems.

So, here I am, 1,200 miles from home, curled up under a U.S. Government- issue green wool blanket and there's a nice kid from New "Joisey" in the next bunk. The plane ride wasn't all that bad. Now that I'm safely on the ground, I hope she was on my flight after all.

Temporary Quarters

We hit the road the evening we were married. I was in the Air Force stationed at Fairchild AFB a few miles out of Spokane, Washington and I had to report back to duty in a week. We arrived in Spokane with no place to stay so we spent our first night at a Holiday Inn and went apartment hunting the next morning.

We found a place rather easily. It was in an old neighborhood not far from the banks of the Spokane river. I'm not sure if the apartments were carved out of a once very large home, or if they were built into the structure. Ours was long and narrow. You walked up a few cement stairs to a small porch. The front door opened into a small ante room with a coat closet. A turn to the right took you into the living room furnished with typical late Fifties blond mahogany chairs end tables and a couch covered in forest green fabric. Further on was the dining room which contained no furniture other than a dark mahogany chest of drawers. The room's most notable feature was its gloominess. The light from the front window exhausted itself before it got this far into the apartment.

At the end of this room was the bedroom, a dark, narrow, almost foreboding chamber. The double bed and dresser left little room for getting around. The most disturbing thing about it was a door that led out onto a wooden porch with stairs that led down to the back yard of the property. The door itself had glass panes covered by laced curtains; the doorknob was cut glass, testimony to a more elegant past. The overall effect was a little Poe-ish and discomfited the young bride. I would not have been surprised to hear a raven rapping at our chamber door. The a small bathroom had standard fixtures including a claw foot bathtub like the one we had in our house when I was a boy.

The best room was the kitchen, decent-sized with functional appliances. Like the living room it was well lit and the kitchen table was situated so you could look out on to the sloping back yard bordered by shrubbery and small trees just where the ground began its decent to the river bank. We never ventured beyond this natural barrier so don't know just how steep it was and where a poor tumbling soul would come to rest. In winter, when the lawn was covered in snow, we would see the occasional quail family skitter across on their way to the sheltering brush.

The front of our apartment was at ground level, but because the building resided on a slope, the kitchen was well above ground. There were apartments next to us on both the ground and upper levels, but ours had no upstairs neighbors. There was a communal laundry room in a centrally located basement. Mr. Peebles, the handy man, was a pleasant older gentleman who tended to begin his day slightly pickled, He was often in the area of the basement and never bothered anyone to our knowledge. My wife found him to be helpful, cordial and always respectful. Looking back through a Twenty first century lens, I marvel at his ability to keep his job. He must have been much loved by the boss. All in all, it was a reasonably comfortable place within our meager budget.

Next door, lived the landlady, a middle-aged widow who

Clueless In Paradise

shared her living space with an aged mother and a young adult daughter of questionable prospects. Once a month my wife took the rent check to her and visited her a while. The landlady seemed to have a warm spot in her heart for the young bride and her Airman husband.

It was mid-winter when we moved in and my wife had seen snow only on trips to the local mountain resorts within an hour or so drive from her family's Southern California home. The first time she looked out the window and saw large, fluffy snowflakes drifting down she put on her coat and gloves and ran outside to play. The charm wore off over time. One morning we awoke to the sound of a snowplow and looked out to see our car half buried in the beautiful stuff. I was going to be late to the base if I didn't get going so the poor dear found herself helping me push the car away from the curb so the tires could grab the road. And she was pregnant.

    With the pregnancy, her first time a long way from home and our financial constraints, (believe it or not, an Airman 2nd Class doesn't earn much money), as well as my crazy work schedule as an Air Police security guard, which left her alone many afternoons and nights, Terri often slipped into a blue mood. We managed to squeeze in some entertainment; the local drive-in movie theater offered a special deal of one dollar per car once you had purchased a full price ticket. We were able to have at least one night out once or twice a month for only a buck. If her spirit sank too low, we might pay a visit to the nearby five and dime store and buy her a trinket. All these years later she has it with her other trinkets and memorabilia, still.

Food was not a problem. My salary and our marriage allotment were sufficient to keep our bellies full. We could stock up on groceries for very little money as long as we stuck to things like pasta, vegetables and cheaper cuts of meat. If you've never eaten a fried potato sandwich with butter, you haven't lived. And there was always the pasta, my heart's delight. One time Terri came home from the base exchange with a mountain of the stuff. It seems one of our air crew had been in Italy and scored a ton of spaghetti which the base was able to sell for eleven cents a pound. Imagine our delight! It wasn't long before my weight reached a level I had never seen.

On our wedding day I weighed in at a paltry one hundred and forty-one pounds. Within a year I was up to an unheard of hundred and seventy-five. To this day, decades later, I've only exceeded that by five pounds, and not for long. The birth of our daughter changed our lives as you would expect. Unfortunately it also changed the lives of the neighbors, our landlady and her aged mother to be exact. Our daughter was a cranky baby and we were new parents, young, inexperienced and a long way from home. To make matters worse, my job required me to go from swing shift to midnight shift to day shift. And the shifts were each only three days long. Lack of sleep, Unhappy baby, dreary bedroom (baby was housed in the dark dining room) and... you get the picture.

Because I feared for the security of my new family, I thought it wise to teach my wife how to shoot a gun. I had a twelve-gauge shotgun I used for bird hunting so I took her to the country to learn its proper and safe use. She did well considering she had never fired a weapon before this. We decided that when I was gone overnight on midnight shifts she should sleep with it beside her, fully loaded. One morning

Clueless In Paradise

a few weeks later, I arrived home to find a clearly shaken young woman. I asked what had happened and she told me that she awakened during the night to the sound of the bedroom door rattling as though someone was trying to turn the knob. (The lovely cut glass knob referred to above.) She said she could see the knob wiggling in the dim light and was terrified. So what did you do? I asked her. Nothing, she said, I was too frightened to move and forgot the gun was even there! I comforted her and relieved her of the weapon immediately, figuring that if anyone got shot it was more likely to be me coming home late from a swing shift.

We had made friends with a few of the neighbors by now. The couple who lived next door could have passed for Midwesterners, so rosy-cheeked and wholesome were they. Madge and Dale were outgoing and amazingly cheery, given the grim weather conditions nine months of the year. Terri and Madge quickly became pals; Dale and I found common ground in short order. He was learning to play the banjo and held Flatt and Scruggs of The Foggy Mountain Boys fame in high regard.

Shortly after we met them they bought a new Chevrolet Corvair convertible. They loved driving with the top down on sunny days, their little pet dog appropriately decked out in travel gear. All these traits would have driven me nuts under different circumstances, but their friendship and companionship were welcome nonetheless. Our friendship even survived my inability to remain awake when they visited us with a baby gift for our newborn daughter. I remember sitting with them in our living room and there being something about a gift. The next thing I remember is Terri poking me in ribs and telling me how rude I had been while they were there.

Sam Culotta

    A few months later we became friends with the couple who lived above Dale and Marge. David, another airman, and his wife Carla, had a little girl about our daughter's age which sealed the deal. Dave and I enjoyed hunting, (an activity I came to abhor a few years later), and we did some bird hunting on land owned by our landlady. I learned quickly that while I enjoyed the process of bagging the birds, I couldn't stand eating them. Terri had never cooked game birds and the first time she cooked a brace of quail the experience was less than pleasant. They smelled funny, were tough and tasted, what else, gamey. Carla once cooked up a batch of dove breasts in some sort of gravy and invited us to the feast. They were a little more palatable than the quail but nothing like chicken.
    David convinced me to buy a rifle suitable for deer hunting. I had no desire to shoot a deer but was willing to give it a try. I bought a war surplus, bolt action German Mauser and the game was afoot. We drove to the country where we gathered our guns and ammo and laid the plans for the hunt. Since I'd never gone after deer I followed Dave's instructions. "Here's what we'll do. You go that way, I'll go this way, and if one of us sights a deer the other will know by the gunshot. If we see nothing, we'll meet back here in an hour."
"Sounds good."

Off we went. I wandered aimlessly knowing chances were very poor I would see anything and secretly hoping I would not. It was a pleasant day and I enjoyed being out in the fresh air feeling the breeze, listening to the chirps of nature. After what seemed like a reasonable amount of time had passed I began to work my way back toward the meeting place. I saw nothing and I heard no gunshots.

Clueless In Paradise

When we met up I reported my lack of results and described a particularly nice spot I had found at the far end of the property when I stopped to have a smoke. "I know" he said, "I watched you through my scope." That marked the end of my hunting activities with David. I'm glad I wasn't wearing antlers at the time.

As Bob Dylan sings in "Tangled Up in Blue", "one day the axe just fell." I returned home from the base one day to find my wife in tears, broken hearted. She had gone next door to pay the monthly rent and that kind middle-aged lady coldly informed her that we had thirty days to vacate the apartment. Our daughter's crying disturbed her mother thus endangering her health. My wife, young and inexperienced in the ways of the world, was caught off guard and took it as a personal rejection by a lady her mother's age, a type who had never been anything but sweet and kind to her all her life.

Finding another apartment was as easy as finding the first one. Within a week we came upon a very nice place in a subdivided house only a few blocks from where we were living. There was an available apartment upstairs and the owner, another very nice, middle-aged widow allowed us to move in as soon as we were able. This place was more modern, cheerier and better furnished. The rent was comparable and the baby's crying would bother no one. The only drawback was that, being upstairs, the summer heat made for some uncomfortable nights.

There were two little problems: the assignment was for one year and I had only nine months of duty remaining and I had no intention of leaving my wife and daughter. To take the posting I would have to extend my enlistment three months. Three months! the sergeant said... only three damn months, and the Air Force will pay for your move back home when

you get discharged! How can you pass that up? Easy.
   Around this time the trouble in Viet Nam was building and was moving inexorably toward U.S. military involvement. There were rumors that all military extensions might be extended to accommodate the forces for a military buildup. President Lyndon Johnson was scheduled to go give a news conference on national television to speak to the nation about the growing threat. Rumor had it he would address the matter of extensions. The morning of the president's speech, Terri and I watched nervously. We had such a short time to go and this could affect our lives in unimaginable ways. He did not announce plans for extension of enlistments.

The final months of my enlistment were some of the best in my life up to that time. When I only had a month or so to go I fell prey to that most wonderful of all physical ailments known as "short-timer's pains". As any GI knows, these are imaginary attacks of very sharp pain that can bring you to your knees. I got mine at the darndest times: right in the middle of a conversation or while walking along with my pals on the way to guard mount I might suddenly double up in mock pain and drop to my knees. "What's wrong?" "Short pains, man...short-timer's pains." Groans from the guys around me. "Want a smoke?" "Nah, I don't have enough time to finish it." Great fun, it was, especially when the victim was a new troop who had no clue.
   Processing out entailed a physical and a dental check. The physical was intended to make sure you were not entitled to post-active duty payment for a disability incurred while serving. I had lost a bit of hearing in my right ear that stemmed

Clueless In Paradise

from an incident on the firing range when the clown beside me fired off his .45 caliber pistol right beside my head. My ear rang for days and I never got all my hearing back. (To this day I use my left ear for telephone conversations.) When I took the hearing test I pointed this out. Although the technician agreed there was some hearing loss, he did not deem it worthy of compensation. They also detected what they called a heart murmur, but did not consider that a problem either. It did scare the hell out of me so to prove to myself I didn't have a bad heart I went to the park with Terri and our little girl and ran around like a madman. Since I didn't vapor-lock and die, I figured I was probably fine.

My remaining time was spent preparing for my discharge, Because our little VW would not hold much beyond our small family and some household goods, we arranged for Terri's parents to drive up from Los Angeles with a borrowed station wagon to help us transport our belongings. They arrived a few days before I was set free so we were packed and ready by the time I drove home from the base for the last time August 9, 1965.The radio was playing Bob Dylan's "Like A Rolling Stone" and I was leaving Fairchild AFB a civilian.

The next day the caravan containing my young family and all our belongings drove up Sunset Hill and on toward home.

Oh, The Waters

> All day I hear the noise of waters
> Making moan,
> Sad as the sea-bird is when, going
> Forth alone,
> He hears the winds cry to the water's
> Monotone.
>
> James Joyce

Passing through northwestern Montana on our way back from Glacier National Park one year, we found ourselves driving along the shore of Flathead Lake. It was a typical grey day for that part of the country. (I spent a few years in Spokane, Washington and am well acquainted with grey days.) The lake appeared grim, the ever present wind blew up white caplets on the iron-cold water. Later summer, and I felt a distinct chill in my bones. No offense intended to the good people of the region; it's more a matter of my long and uneasy relationship with bodies of water. Lakes, oceans, rivers and their waterfalls have often visited my dreams, and I've never enjoyed their visits.

    My earliest recollections are of our family visits to the shores of Lake Ontario in Rochester, N.Y. The shore we frequented was called Charlotte Lake and had about as safe a beach area as you could imagine. I remember as a small boy, unable to swim, I could wade out a very long way without getting in too deep. The bottom was scored by semi-permanent shingles of sand. There were other areas along the

Clueless In Paradise

shoreline where the water was deeper and where my parents and uncles engaged in aquatic horseplay. We kids hung out a little closer to shore and floated in inner tubes under the vigilant eye of monitors. One day an uncle, given to stupid behavior, decided I should know how to swim, and dunked me. Another uncle took umbrage and almost drowned him. This was my first experience with the downside of water play.

Our beach areas usually closed down by late summer due to water pollution. We would arrive filled with excitement only to see dead fish floating by. The sign would read: "Closed To Swimmers". It was believed that polluted water, among other things, could cause polio, the scourge of our summers.

Forward a couple of years to the time our egg man missed his delivery. When he showed up the next week we learned that his son had been wading in the lake, fell into a deep hole and drowned. One winter's night the phone rang while we were eating dinner. My mother answered it in another room but we could tell by her voice that the news was not good. After a few minutes she returned to the kitchen and announced that a friend of the family had called to say their son had drowned in the school's indoor pool while practicing with his swim team. The coach told the family that after a practice lap he noticed a boy missing and found their son at the bottom of the pool.

One winter my Godmother's son joined a gymnasium and convinced my mother it would be good for me to go with him. We could meet at the bus stop and ride together. I was reluctant to do it; I was, and am, averse to clubs and group activities. (I joined the Cub Scouts one summer and lasted only until the picnic where I was welcomed as a Tenderfoot.) But my mother felt obligated which meant I was, so off I went, filled with trepidation. The sessions began around five p.m. which meant it was already getting dark by the time we got there. We began with some harmless exercises on the gym floor that lasted about twenty minutes, then were sent back to the locker room to strip down and go to the pool. This was the part I hated. No swimsuits, just a bunch of bare butt boys lined up in the staircase while we waited for the older class to vacate the pool area. When they did, they took great delight in stinging us with their wet towels as they passed by. Long story short, after two or three weeks of this my mother could tell I was miserable and let me quit.

    What sealed the deal for me was a family trip to Niagara Falls when I was about ten. We made a fun stop at the Buffalo Zoo where I saw a silver python sleeping contentedly after having swallowed lunch. This was obvious from the way the meal altered the python's otherwise svelte figure. I mention this because all these years later the image remains vivid despite the sensory experience that lay ahead.

    Niagara Falls is awe inspiring by any measure. We came first to the Niagara river. It flows cold and fast, full to the banks, exuberant as a young bull racing into the bull ring. Already we could hear the deep rumble of the cataract and the closer we came to it the louder it became. We saw where the river flowed over the edge and we reached the observation area where we stood amazed; the monstrous power and brute force of the falls created a noise so thunderous as to intimidate conversation. The land we stood on trembled. I could not watch without imagining myself tumbling off the ledge to certain death. A few years later we learned that the earth where we stood had crumbled away, victim to the falls' relentless roar.

Clueless In Paradise

  The physical and visual sensations were imprinted in my brain for all time. To this day, decades later, I have dreams of driving into unfamiliar areas that are suddenly covered with water, or find myself walking along a rushing river afraid I'll slip off into it. Events have contributed to my discomfort.
  When I was fifteen, my mother, sister and I went back to Rochester by train for a visit. It was an adventure I loved for the most part. At one point, the railroad tracks cross the Ohio River. I say "cross" the river, but to the eye of an unsuspecting fifteen year old traveler it appeared to cross ON the river. All I could see was a vast expanse of grey water to either side and that all too familiar horror scurried up my spine like an alley rat. And again, a few years later a group of us stayed with a friend's family at their beach house in Southern California. I got up during the night to use the bathroom but didn't want to walk through the mother's bedroom to get there, so opted for the vast sandy beach. When I stepped outside, the ocean was almost at the back door; the tide had come in when I wasn't looking. I stifled a shriek, took care of business with dispatch and got the hell back in as fast as I could.
  When I was in the Air Force a few of us went on a late night fishing trip through the mountain roads outside Spokane, Washington. As we came around a sharp bend the headlights of our car illuminated an icy, black river gleaming in the moonlight. For a few moments we all gasped, (or maybe it was only me), thinking we were about to drive right into it.
  I hate to place the blame for all this on my late beloved mother but when I was a boy, she and I would walk to Rochester's downtown area. We had to cross the bridge over the Genesee River hundreds of feet below. She made me take the rail because she was afraid. She was also terrified of

mountains, so much so as to cause my father to take the longer "southern route" when we crossed the country to settle in California. This route avoided the more direct and popular scenic route that crossed the Rocky Mountains. Of course, where we ended up living was near the foothills of the San Gabriel mountains, a fact she brought up to my father often for the rest of their lives.

    Recently, my wife, sister, brother-in-law and I went back east for my Uncle's surprise 90th birthday celebration. Of course while there we were obliged to go see "the Falls" as they call them. It's only a seventy-two mile drive from Rochester, a mere side trip for Southern Californians. The place was crowded; ever a tourist attraction it drew people from all over the world. We lined up at the rail to view the spectacular beauty of the beast that ate the shoreline. But this time I wasn't uncomfortable. Maybe it was the different perspective from our vantage point, maybe it was familiarity since this was my third visit. Anyhow, I've had no bad dreams since that visit three years ago. Let's hope it stays that way.

No Sweat

A couple of months ago, Terri and I decided to join a fitness center. I've been threatening to do this for a very long time. In fact, I weighed much less when the notion first struck me; since then, I've gained at least fifteen pounds so it's about time I did something about it. Terri has done a great job of getting her weight down but is desirous of strengthening her legs and of improving her cardio-vascular capacity or, as we gym rats refer to it, her "cardio". So when we learned that our Medicare-plus healthcare provider covers one hundred percent of gym memberships in selected facilities, we realized we had run out of excuses and we joined. The price was right.

Terri isn't interested in the exercise equipment that concentrates on all the important muscle groups; she is happy to prop her Kindle in front of her and pedal or walk on the appropriate apparatus for about an hour. We manage to go together twice a week and I manage to go once more on my own usually. I do about fifteen minutes on the bicycle or treadmill and then move on to the weight machines. I began thinking I too wanted to improve my cardio above all else, but I've begun to grow fond of the machines and of the notion that I can tone up my aging body enough to draw envious looks from passing jocks and fit young women. Vanity really is the last thing to go.

While there are a fair number of mature folks in the gym these days, due to the fact that membership is free, I guess, the great percentage of members are young. I thought there would be a certain amount of camaraderie given the close quarters and the fact that the activities are conducive to a sense of well being, but not really. The older folks seem dour and the younger ones are either too caught up in their exertions, imprisoned by the media outlets plugged into their ears, or both, to bother being friendly. I can understand why the young women avoid contact; gyms are, after all, meat markets. The male, drawn by the rich scent of the female in close quarters, abetted by a luxuriant effusion of his own hormones, might take the merest bit of eye contact as sexual invitation. I remember that when I worked in downtown Los Angeles, the fear of eye contact was just as critical for women, and the only effusion there was cheap aftershave, so I may be underestimating the female's awareness of danger.

    I notice this aversion to human intercourse most where the bicycle and treadmill machines are lined up side by side. The proximity here can be a bit discomfiting, especially if the person next you is thumping away at a jog or running sideways for whatever the hell reason a person runs sideways. It can be distracting as well. One of the first times I ever used the treadmill I was walking along minding my own business, trying to avoid looking at my neighbor, when I saw something out of the corner of my eye. I didn't want to break the "code" so I resisted looking for as long as I could. When I gave in and turned my head I saw that the young lady on my right was stretching, I guess to warm-up before she began her walk/jog, and that her left foot was on the very top of the machine. Her other leg was exactly where it should have been, directly beneath her. I was amazed that she could get her leg up that high and was about to tell her that if I tried that I'd have to have EMT standing by, but stifled myself just in time to

Clueless In Paradise

avoid an embarrassing breach of gym decorum.

Upstairs, where the fancy stuff is, the atmosphere is about the same but the people watching opportunities are much better. When you're seated at a machine you can watch and be watched by others. They truly represent an impressive range of shapes, sizes and, like standing at a urinal trough in the restroom of a sports stadium. you are forced to look straight ahead at a bare, blank tile wall, or risk the ultimate embarrassment of causing your neighbor to think you're checking out his equipment. Ironically, unless you have a particularly pointed interest in said equipment it's the last thing on earth you want to see.

When gym rats perform their routines there is only one person on their minds and only one person they care to ogle: that person is themselves. Gyms have an abundance of mirrors. The theory is that it's important for the lifter to observe his or her body as it goes through its motions and thereby insure they are performing the routine correctly. It's a convenient theory for those who just love to watch their muscles contract and expand. I have tried it on the few occasions in which I've used free weights, but watching myself embarrasses me. I don't find my seventy year-old sinews and ligaments all that attractive and I am especially put off by the grimaces I make lifting the weights over my head. It is far more pleasant to watch the reflected image of a twenty-something young lady beside me doing contortions on an exercise ball. But back to the machines.

I mentioned the impressive range of body types on display in these places. A few days ago I was comfortably moving thirty pounds back and forth on the "chest press" machine when a real serious workout denizen of the club arrived. I appreciate a well-muscled body as much as the next guy, but this fellow had worked his oh so humble mortal coil into a shape that must make even his mother avert her eyes. There is not a spare inch of flesh on this man that isn't on the verge of tearing open from the knotted mass beneath it. There are muscles in his eyelids! Like a victim of a Botox overdose, his face is frozen in a grimace resembling a smile but absent the mirth. His arms have not touched his sides in many a moon. It hurts to look at him.

Then, while I continue to build my "pecs", another man arrives. This man is older than I am, maybe a decade older, he is long and lean; his limbs are thin and lanky and his skin resembles that of raw poultry. He sits at the chest/back exercise machine almost directly across from me and goes to work pushing and pulling with little sign of exertion. I figured the old guy was pumping twenty or thirty pounds and I gave him high marks for his grit and for his determination to maintain his health at such an advanced stage because it's not doing much for his physique.. When he left I went to take a look and saw that the weight was set at 160 pounds!

The gym has an Olympic-sized swimming pool, a spa and a sauna. I haven't taken advantage of any of these yet because I'm not comfortable with the whole locker room scene. I spent some time going to boys' gymnasiums as a child and there were high school sports and my four year stint in the Air Force, so my reluctance isn't due to misplaced modesty. Still, I find it distasteful at this stage of my life so I'm holding off on taking the plunge. Every time I walk by the pool on my way upstairs to work with the machines I wish I was in there swimming; it's the showering and re-dressing that put me off. One day soon I'll do it. It didn't help that the first time I walked through the locker room I was treated to the unsightly sight of a man bending over to pull up his underwear. Maybe

Clueless In Paradise

once that image fades away I'll give it a try.

It would help if I could sweat easily. I ran into a couple of neighbor ladies when I was working out one day and they were sweating profusely. They wore sweat bands and had towels draped over their shoulders. Their faces were flushed and their shirts sported blots of perspiration. After we exchanged pleasantries, one asked me if I was working out or just visiting. I said I'd been working out for about forty-five minutes. She said I must not be working out very hard because I wasn't even sweating. My dirty secret was out: I don't sweat much. It has to be very hot and humid, and I have to work awfully hard to get wet, and even then, the most I produce are a few patches of perspiration here and there. On rare occasions I will generate enough moisture to cause a small rivulet of sweat to run down my face. So, although I'd been grunting and groaning, I was only modestly flushed. If you were curious enough to touch my skin you would find it moist and warm. Sorry, but it's the best I can do. I do carry a towel with me when I'm there, more out of sense of duty than anything else.

There is an accepted rule of gym behavior that requires you to wipe down a machine when you finish with it out of consideration for the person who uses it next. Once in a while I use my towel to "mop" my face or neck because it feels kind of nice and also because it makes it look as though I need to. I keep a water bottle with me; I may not sweat a lot but I do get thirsty and I believe in keeping myself hydrated, and it's handy to have because I can splash some water on my shirt as I'm coming down the stairs to the main floor just in case I run into the ladies again.

I've been at this for a little over two months now and I can report some notable results: my biceps, triceps and deltoids are showing definite signs of improvement. I can push, pull or lift greater amounts of weight than I did when I started. It's not all good, though; when I began doing this I weighed one hundred and eighty one pounds. As of my last weigh-in I had lost one pound. People tell me that is to be expected because I'm adding muscle which is heavier than the fat I'm burning off. I'm not convinced that is not just a form of self talk used by long-suffering gymsters to convince themselves that all the grunting and groaning is worth it somehow. I don't know how much more of this I can take but I'd sure like to persist until I can keep up with Superman's grandfather over there.

Captain Contrary

Growing up in my neighborhood, everything was a contest. We argued over who was the greater cowboy, Roy Rogers or Gene Autry. Roy Rogers was the favorite but I preferred Gene Autry. I don't remember whether I liked him better because the others liked Rogers, or if I actually preferred Autry. Roy Rogers was dashing, he had his pretty wife, Dale, and his golden palomino, Trigger. Gene Autry was more homey; his horse was a chestnut named Traveler. He had no female companion, just a collection of sourdoughs and they sat around the bunk house or camp fire singing songs and sharing one hotdog or one donut (I specifically recall a scene with them cutting a donut into pieces because it was all the grub they had), until someone came riding up at a gallop shouting, "Gene, Gene! There's some rustlers stealing Mr Jones' cattle and he sent me to ask for your help!" Then Gene would put down his guitar and tell the boys to saddle up and get riding, there were bad guys to fight.

Roy Rogers looked just a bit too smug and happy. Dale was a sweetheart and boon companion, Trigger was a show horse and Gabby Hayes was a salty old sidekick who provided comic relief. The arrangement was just too wholesome for my tastes. Rogers also would do a bit of trick riding in his movies and I remember using his stunt of standing up on Trigger as rhetorical ammo because he kept his spurs on and that must have been tough on the poor horse.

Sam Culotta

Life has a funny way of recycling the past. Years later on a drive to Laughlin, Nevada, we passed the Roy Rogers Museum in Victorville, California. Out where passersby could see it was a giant statue of Trigger rearing up on his hind legs, as iconic a pose as ever was. We didn't pay it much attention until a time later when my father was with us. He knew about the museum and he was on the alert to see Trigger. "Hey, keep an eye out for Trigger! He's coming up pretty soon!" And as we passed it he'd get a big grin on his face and remark as to what a beautiful horse that was.

Most of the kids on my block were Yankees fans. The Yanks were winning World Series with disgusting regularity. Our local AAA Rochester Red Wings were the farm team of the St. Louis Cardinals and many of our players went up there. Some stuck, some came back to live out their careers with the Red Wings. My favorite player was Eddie Mierkowicz, the center fielder. He was a big hunk of a guy who hit well and had great power. He went up to the big club and returned a couple of times but was expected to make it for keeps one day soon. Then he got beaned. Took one right square in the temple. This was before the baseball helmet so there was nothing to protect him but his baseball cap. The paper reported that he was rushed to the hospital where he underwent two hours of surgery, (two hours under the knife, is how they put it). Although he returned after a long rehab, he was not the player he had been and never did make it to the majors.

One summer around this time a kid showed up on the street, a cousin of one of our neighbor kids, visiting from Brooklyn, N.Y.. Blond and arrogant, he had an annoying Brooklynese accent and a bad case of attitude. Talked to us like the big city mouse visiting his poor country cousins. I would

Clueless In Paradise

argue with him over the relative qualities of his Dodgers and my Red Wings. One of his bragging points was that the Dodgers players had white satin home uniforms that glistened under the lights at night games. I couldn't top that. Eventually, I became a Dodger fan and remain one to this day. Our family moved to L.A. in 1953. At that time Los Angeles had two AAA Pacific Coast League (PCL) baseball teams: the Los Angeles Angels, who played at Wrigley Field near downtown, and the Hollywood Stars who played at Gilmore Stadium located not far The teams were bitter rivals; more than a few games featured fisticuffs. I remember the Stars' Bobby Bragan and the Angels' Gene Mauch (later the manager of the major league Angels) getting into it a few times.

    I discovered that a big ol' first baseman named Steve Bilko was playing for the Angels. Bilko had been one of my favorite players with the Red Wings so I immediately became an Angels fan. Big Bilko was a powerhouse minor leaguer who went up and down to the Cardinals, and later, the Cubs for a few years, but really found a home in Los Angeles. In 1956 he won the PCL Triple Crown hitting .360, blasting 55 home runs and driving in 164 runs. He was later inducted into the PCL Hall of Fame. It was great fun while it lasted but even greater fun was on the way. The Brooklyn Dodgers announced their move to Los Angeles in 1958. The rest is history.

    My father was a crack auto mechanic. He hated Fords because they were, in his words, "a bitch to work on". So, despite their immense popularity I, like him, was a Chevy guy. When Dad crossed me up and bought a used, late 40's, Studebaker I resisted switching to a car I'd never even heard of before. He had owned a Packard at one time also. What can I say? He was a man in constant search of excellence. Eventually, he bought a 1951 Nash Rambler Station Wagon and drove us across country to California. What kid goes around bragging that his dad owns a Nash Rambler? Nash was best known for its "upside down bathtub" design in those days, a huge boat that looked very much as it was characterized. The Rambler was at least more compact and almost attractive in an entomologic sort of way. He went on to buy a Nash Statesman, another huge vehicle best remembered as the "bedroom on wheels" because of its reclining front seats, certainly a worthwhile advance in automotive design. I was allowed to take it on dates.

I was a good athlete even though I was undersized for my age. My best sport was baseball; I had been playing ball since I could stand and by the time I was in high school I had a few years of competitive softball under my belt. I wasn't a power hitter but I hit for average, had good speed and quickness, sure hands and a strong arm. So of course when I got to high school I went out for the freshman basketball team. I remember the day I signed up. They recorded my weight at a hefty ninety-eight pounds and my height as four feet and eleven inches tall in my tennis shoes.

A guy built like me and with my skills would most likely make a good guard, so I tried out at forward. You see, my best friend was a guard and we had a chemistry. He knew my moves and was good at getting the ball to me. The coach went along with it after he saw us practice a few times. By my Junior year I had shot up to five feet six inches tall, but by then I wasn't playing basketball anymore. By then I was smoking and getting into a lot of trouble at school.

On to college, and couple of dismal semesters later I joined the Air Force. It wasn't my idea exactly; I blame it on the Soviets. Almost as if they knew I was floundering and would be easy pickings, they decided to build that damn Berlin wall between East and West Germany. This prompted President John F. Kennedy to beef up the U.S.'s military presence in that area. To aid in this build-up he announced that, effective immediately, college draft deferments were revoked for students whose grade point averages were below "C". My GPA was below "C" and sinking fast. My friend, Steve, was not in college, so he suggested the time was right for us to enlist. That way we could select the branch of service that would best meet our needs. Our needs were mainly that we remain stateside so we could marry our intended wives and so I could continue my college education while on active duty.

Steve loved airplanes but neither of us wanted to enlist for four years; the Army offered three year enlistments. During our interview with the Army recruiter we learned that chances were over ninety percent we would be sent to Germany. We went next door to the Air Force recruiting office where we were assured there was a very good chance of stateside assignments and a larger selection of career paths.

The enlistment forms included a "wish list". I requested the aforementioned stateside duty and a career choice of medical training, since my woeful college career was in pre-med. I knew that the medical training was held at a tech school in Alabama, which I considered U.S. territory at the time. If memory serves me, Steve asked for air traffic control training. Shortly before our basic training ended the assignments for each of us in our Flight were posted on the wall. We gathered around the notice to see where we were going to be sent. Steve and I couldn't believe our eyes. I was assigned to a nice enough place: Fairchild, AFB outside Spokane, Washington, and Steve was assigned to a base in Blytheville, Arkansas.

Sam Culotta

The bad news: our duty assignment was Air Police, Combat Defense, a euphemism for "security guard". We soon learned it was better known as: "poor bastards who stand on the frozen flight-line to guard hulking B-52 bombers and KC-135 refueling tankers for eight hour shifts which switch every seventy-two hours from day, to swing to midnight shift."

I sat on the edge of my cot numb with disappointment. Across from me was a large young man who was almost in tears. I asked him how he was doing. He told me he was heartbroken; he was hoping to be an Air Policeman and got some crap assignment as a medic. I can't say this made me feel any better.

My military career was much like my later banking and finance career. I did very well in spite of myself. After a short blip, (I was busted down from Airman 3rd class to Airman Basic for a slight weapons mishap), my fortune improved rapidly and I left the service an Airman 1st class, a rank many of my buddies didn't reach. To be honest, the competition is not all that great. If you test well, pass the Canadian Five BX exercise program, shoot straight (thanks Dad, for taking me hunting a lot) and show up with a sharp uniform, success, such as it is, is yours

What this all proves is not clear. Dare to be different? Rely on the kindness of strangers? It's better to be lucky than good? I've been thinking about this for at least fifty years now, (I discount my twenties when I was not thinking about much at all), and I have no answers. I do suspect, however, that life is much simpler than we think. We complicate things; it's our nature to do so. Every time I needed it, luck or a burst of inspiration or the support of someone I felt least likely to

Clueless In Paradise

help, turned up to save me and propel me along. I wish I had a better answer but many years of thought on the subject reveals nothing more to me. Still, I'm open for suggestions.

How I Learned To Speak Italian Incorrectly

My Italian-Sicilian parents, grandparents, aunts, uncles, cousins and goombadies, (see below), were, well, loquacious, to put it mildly. They were often bombastic, and gatherings could get raucous. Colorful language was delivered with remarkable zest, opinions half-baked but delivered hot from the oven, curses, blessings, shouts of anger and love. It could be unsettling for a kid, but never dull.

I have attempted to compile a collection of the tastier words and phrases I heard; some caustic enough to peel paint, some bursting with flavor like a mouthful of mom's meatballs, some savory, some bitter. My little lexicon of terms begins with the way they sounded to me and what I understood them to mean, followed by the correct spelling and meaning. Sicilian Italian, like that of other regions of Italy, has its own peculiarities. If, dear reader, you disagree with my pronunciations and/or meanings, please indulge me.

Angótta : again? still? Yet?
In my experience always expressed in the form of a question as in: "Angotta, Again witta you bigga feet? You banga my legs and hurts me honey!"

"Sorry Grandma."

Years later I learned it's actually *encóre* as in: "They want an encore." "They did it again."

Átchitoo!: God bless you. No, it's not a sneeze; it's something that my parents' generation seemed to have a lot of. They would say things like: *Dio*, that sausage gave me atchitoo.

Found out it's actually **ácito**: (pronounced, aggita) ... sour, acidic. It was something I associated with elderly people. (I could eat a bucketful of pasta without the slightest bit of discomfort.) Years later when I was in the Air Force standing guard on a midnight shift, I was taken to the chow hall for the one meal they were obligated to provide us. I ate rubbery scrambled eggs, lukewarm fried potatoes, and a banana, topped off with coffee that must have been strained through King Kong's jockstrap, followed by a couple of unfiltered cigarettes. And, it was only one A.M.! About thirty minutes later I felt like my esophagus was disgorging lava. Damn if I wasn't experiencing my first achitoo attack! I had become an adult.
Note: The terms, aggitto or aggitta, are used by some. This may be a colloquial use of the word for agitated or upset: *agitate.*

Basta! Enough! Stop!
By now, almost everyone knows what this means. *Basta* is one of the great Italian expressions, as is *acito* or *aggitta*. (See atchitoo, above.)

I thought they were saying pasta and I couldn't figure out why they were so mad. Since it was almost always the men, I thought maybe they were mad because their wives hadn't served the pasta in time. Occasionally, I'd hear something like, " pasta butahn". A particular type of pasta, I thought. Crude though they were, this was not used often, and no explanation was ever forthcoming; I had to watch an old Italian movie to learn it was actually *basta puttana:* Enough, whore!

In defense of my people I should point out that they came from a heritage in which the man of the family ruled with an iron fist. When disputes or carping occurred during gatherings, most often meals, the father might get tired of hearing it and use this term, accompanied by a hand slam to the table top, to shut up his wife or children and restore order. The fact that it was usually meal time may be why I thought he was calling for pasta.

Bootigia tu namino:

I always interpreted this to mean something like: "Oh, for crying out loud!" or, "For Pete's sake". But I knew something was wrong because when a woman in our family used it, (and it seemed to be something used more often by the women), it always caused a slight uplift of the eyebrows and maybe a giggle from the others.
"Mom, are you saying something dirty?" "No, Honey, it just means your grandfather's bottle." And they'd all laugh again. By now, I'm sure you've figured it out.
Bottílgia tuo nonno: Your grandfather's bottle, indeed!

Breezcu: An Italian card game.

Briscula: The Sicilian variation of the Italian game, *Briscola.*

Clueless In Paradise

At family gatherings the men matched up in teams of two for a "friendly" game of *briscula:* We children could only watch. I wasn't allowed to participate until I was well into my teens, and then only when they were short a real man.

The game is a relatively simple one of following suit and winning tricks with high card or by using the *briscula,* or trump. The deck of forty cards excludes Jokers, 8's, 9's, and 10's. Ace is high, three is next, (hey, not my rules), then King on down. Ace is 11 points, 3 is 10, King is 4, Queen is 3, Jack is 2, the rest have no points but can capture tricks if they are the highest and/or of the trump suit. Got it?

Now here's the fun part. You see, the generic game rules forbid talking between partners, but the Sicilian version is given it's gusto by a constant flow of hints, jokes, and taunts. This produces some great moments of laughter and some of the most colorful swearing ever to bless the ears of a young boy. And there are signals that the players can use at the risk of their opponents picking them off. There are undoubtedly variations but these which I found on an Italian game site are close to those I remember seeing while camped at my father's side.

> Ace: *(asso)* stretch lips over teeth or purse lips.
> Three: distort mouth to one side.
> King: glance upward or raise eyebrows.
> Queen: shrug one shoulder.
> Jack: show the tip of the tongue or lick lips.
> Threes or Aces outside of the *Briscula* suit - quickly open and close your mouth.

I also remember them using an eye blink (Ace), and puffed cheek for the three, but I could be wrong. They referred to the ace as *asso*, which sounded like ewzo to my ears, and to the three of trump as something that sounded like goddico. I loved this word because my Irish uncle pronounced it gaddiker which set them all howling with laughter. (He also pronounced *cannoli*, canoller. Poor guy was the only non-Italian in the family at the time.)

    These relatively unsophisticated, unschooled men could keep track of the cards as well as any casino gambler. Grandpa, who signed documents with an "X", would sit there like he was uninterested but pick off his opponents' signs while sending his own with complete success. When I grew up and he was still living with us, we would play two man *briscula* and try as I might, I could never stop him from knowing the final three cards in my hand, something that made him chuckle with quiet self-satisfaction.

Butahna: Whore, prostitute.
Puttána: Whore, prostitute. See *Basta* above for one of its applications. This pejorative was not just used to insult women. To illustrate: A woman might (and did) snap at a man and call him *figlio puttane*, or son of a whore. This sort of curse had to be used with great care because Italian men often have difficulty separating an insult to them from an insult to their sainted mamas. This could lead to a real ugly scene.

    Side note: My father was not easily shocked and certainly could dish it out as well as the next guy, but, one curse word set him off big time. If you called him a son-of-a-bitch, he took it as an insult to his mother and then, look out.

Clueless In Paradise

Coleóni: Except for the fact that the men used this term when they were, well, being men, I would have thought this was an Italian pastry, like *cannoli,* and since this was years before Mario Puzzo even thought of writing The Godfather, it couldn't mean Don Corleone.

Coglióne: Balls (testicles), asshole, dickhead. In defense of my particular family, they used it more for balls than for the other meanings. But I could be wrong.

Coogóotz: I never got the feeling that this was a bad word, just a slang term for someone who was a jerk. When I asked what it meant I got the usual dust-off: "oh, it means squash, zucchini."

Cucúzza: Literally, a big squash. When used as an insult or criticism it means someone who is worthless as a big, dumb vegetable. It doesn't differ much from *citrullo*, (see below) but rather than calling someone a dumbbell, you're calling them a useless lump. A difference without a distinction?

Cornúto: Literally, horned (as a goat), but the most common usage is to characterize a man as a cuckold. This is considered the worst possible insult in the Italian language; it means more than the fact that your wife is cheating on you, it also infers that you are either too stupid or too timid to challenge the man who is cuckolding you. And, if that were not enough, it infers you are not man enough to satisfy and control your woman. Fighting words? More like killing words. The first time I was made aware of this word was when I saw the movie, *Rose Tattoo*, starring Anna Magnani and Burt Lancaster. I remember a scene where the children of the village trailed the star's husband making the sign of the goat, a way of telling him he was a cornúto. Much storming and threats of violence follow, often leading to violence itself.

Note: not to be confused with the harmless word, *cardoon* or as I heard it: gardoona, which is a vegetable. A colloquial word for the Cardi,(chard), botanical *compare* to the artichoke. Its stringy, reddish stalks are tricky to prepare but are a favorite of Italian cooks.

Dástadútta: Stubborn, hard-headed. Men used it to describe their wives and sometimes their children, although, women were quite free with the term as well.
Tésta dúro: I didn't realize it was a two word phrase, but I did get the meaning.

Disgráziato: Disgusting, wretched, disgraceful. See *miserabile*, below.

Gabéesh. Understand? Get it? Can you dig it? The latter term would seem to be the one that has been bastardized for general consumption.
Capíre : To understand.
Capísce: He, she, it, understands.
Needs no explanation; I'm sure we've all heard or used this word many times.

Goombody, or góoombah.

Clueless In Paradise

This term also needs no explanation. When used by an Italian it is usually a playful expression that refers to a friend or companion. When used by a non-Italian it is often taken as insulting. Gabeesh?

Compáre: Godfather, partner, accomplice.
Comáre : Godmother, gossip, next-door-neighbor.
Notice the subtle but very important gender differences in the secondary meanings,. Very important.

Gitroolu.. I often heard this used when my father made reference to someone he didn't care for, often one of his in-laws. As in: "Oh, him. He's a damn gitroolu, always has been!"

Citrúllo:: dumb
In this case, it worked in reverse. I always assumed from the way he said it that it meant "asshole". Dumb is not so bad.

Mamaluke: Commonly used to characterize someone who was either ignorant or who behaved stupidly. I got the distinct impression my family used it to describe someone who was less than sharp.
Mammalúcco: dolt, idiot
I guess I had this one about right.

Maróne: (pron. *Madón*)
I doubt this requires explanation. It is simply *Madonna* as pronounced in the southern areas of Italy. It can mean *"Holy cow!"* or, *"Holy smokes!"* Nothing really crude or foul because, hey, it's Our Lady!

Méengia: Darn! Wow! (I thought).
A few of my uncles used this word to express dismay or shock as in: Meengia, what a lousy day I'm having!

Minchia : means: What a prick, or holy shit, or WTF!
I discovered this when, as a young man in my twenties and possessed of a bit too much New Year's Eve spirit, I used this word to toast my 85 year old grandmother from across the room. Grandma, whose varicose-veined legs I often kicked as a boy (see *encore* above), let out a shriek and fell backwards off her seat. Thankfully, she laughed at the same time, as did the rest of my family, so no blood was spilt.

Mizerabilah: This is another one that I heard right.
Miserábile: means miserable, of course, but where English speakers use the word as an adjective, Italians often use it as a noun to describe someone who they consider a scoundrel or low life. This explains why it was always used to express disgust, often accompanied by a disgusted look and a string of further insults or curses intended to amplify the meaning, as in: "Bah, *miserabile disgraziato!*" Roughly translated: "you wretched, rotten, miserable low-life!" Pretty effective use of two words.

Moosha- moosh: This is a tricky one. As used in our family it referred to pasta that was overcooked. I can't find a translation for this term or something like it. The Italian word for overcooked is *scotto*, or *stracótto*. But the fact that it may not be in the Italian dictionary doesn't make moosha- moosh any less important a term.

Clueless In Paradise

It can be a bombshell when dropped at the dinner table under the wrong conditions.

Grandma, (*encore!*), who was living with her daughter and my Irish uncle at the time, sparked a short but pyrotechnical family event one Sunday afternoon when she tried to point out to my aunt that my uncle's spaghetti that day was cooked moosha-moosh. My uncle had a heart of gold and doted on my aunt more than any Italian husband would have at the time. He did, however, have a classic Irish temper and when he heard his mother-in-law speak in Italian, especially *sotto voce*, he got disturbed. He didn't know much Italian but he damn sure knew she was complaining about the spaghetti he had cooked.

It was a Sunday afternoon; we were sitting at home minding our own business when the phone rang. After a brief conversation, my mother hung up and told Dad something. He swore, then got us all into the car and headed to my aunt's house only a few blocks away. On the way Mom told us that our aunt had called in a panic because my uncle had lost his temper and was breaking things. She was afraid for herself and for her poor Mama. When we got there she met us on the front lawn and tried to assure us that all had calmed down and to please not mak a big thing about it when we went in to the house. Inside, we found Grandma sitting on the sofa looking perfectly innocent. My uncle was in the kitchen sheepishly washing spaghetti off the wall. *Marone!*

Nápolitana: This one's a little different because it's an actual word, pronounced correctly. The problem was in my interpretation. You see, a Sicilian may say this word like he or she is spitting out something particularly nasty as in :

va'fa Napoli. I can be forgiven for believing it meant something dirty or foul. One day I screwed up my courage and asked what it meant and was told: "Oh, honey, it's not a swear word, it only means someone from Naples, or telling someone to go to Naples. This was my introduction to the lingering hatred of people from other cities left over from the time Italy was a loose collection of city-states. Italians have long memories when it comes to rivalries.

Well, *va'fa Napoli* does mean go to Naples, literally, but as with so many "special" curses it has a far more acidic meaning to the cognoscenti. It can mean something relatively innocent like, "go to hell" but is actually the polite form of *vafanculo*, a suggestion that the recipient experience sodomy. The clever sub-meaning is that Naples was considered by other Italians to be the land of sodomy, so by telling a person to go there...well, you get the picture.

Note: *Abruzziz and Calabriz* were also spat out like bad fava beans but, as I learned later, were only descriptors of natives of Abruzzi and Calabria. There was one of each in our family circle.

Porko lardo: I thought this might be "fat pig". Makes sense.

Porco lordo: Literally, dirty pig. One of those expressions I heard from the women folk more than the men. My mother often used it to describe me when I had been playing outside and got filthy. *Porco* can mean porker or fatso, but it can also be used to deliver a boatload of more pointed insults such as any or all of the following: pig, degenerate, lecher, swine, slime ball or sleaze bag. *Porco puttana*, or dirty whore, was the most vulgar usage of this expression and was

Clueless In Paradise

used sparingly, usually when tempers were very hot. As a person who loves words and word usage, I have a great deal of respect for such a versatile projectile.

Stugotts: Caution: adult language

I admit, this wasn't commonly used but it made an impression because it had that wonderful verbal zest coming out the mouth. I figured it meant something like: you're crazy, or, you're full of shit. Well, if only it had. You see, one day when a friend was visiting and I wanted to show off my cultural chops, I used it to express impatience with him. Unfortunately, my mother was right next to me and my head was in her sweet zone. Wham! She unleashed a forehand that would have made Arthur Ashe envious.

"Where did you hear that word!" she shouted. I took a moment to regain my balance and spoke over the ringing in my ear.
 "Mom, I hear it from my uncles some time." I whined.
"Your uncles would never talk that way in front of you!"
"Well, I didn't make it up!"
"I don't care where you heard it. Don't ever let me hear you say that again."

Tu cazzo: You prick. Cazzo also means: Damn! Shit! Prick and Cock. Mom had every right to knock me silly.

Zooma, zooma baccala.
I'm sure many of you are familiar with the great Louis Prima. He often sang this take off on an old Italian number. It's a humorous and naughty ditty that evoked no end of snickers

Sam Culotta

and guffaws from my relatives. Of course, I could never figure out what was so funny so, years later, I asked my father. What's *zooma, zooma baccala* mean anyway, and why do you guys get such a kick out of it? Since I was a young adult by then, Dad figured I should know. "*Zooma, zooma*", he said and pumped his arm in a piston-like motion which even I could interpret easily. "Oh", I said, 'but what the heck's a *baccala?*" "It's a fish, a cod fish" and he winked. "You get it? You *zooma, zooma* the *baccala*"! Yikes! I get it! *Basta!*

So, there you have it. I'm sure there are more but these are what I remember. I'm also certain that different dialects and family cultures used these words and expressions in their own way. It's important to understand that this sort of banter went on in mixed company and in front of the children. Most of the time the adults were laughing and cutting up when they spoke this way so we kids never got the feeling that something terrible was being said. Very few of my parents' generation are with us now and this language which was woven into the texture of our lives is as much a part of my memories as are the faces and voices of my beloved family.

I Sing The Body Decrepit

I am never alone. A few years ago I developed tinnitus; when all outside sounds are absent it keeps me company. Its high-pitched static whooshes through my head in stereo, the old fashioned kind of stereo that amazed us in its early years, sounding like someone invisible was walking or dancing across the floor. Silence is no longer a part of my life and while it irritated me for a long time, I've learned to accept it the way you learn to accept the presence of someone who just won't take the hint and leave. It's not a friend, exactly, but I'm sure I would miss it if it were to disappear suddenly. I'm not complaining; it could be worse, much worse. My poor departed mother suffered her entire life from hearing loss and blindness in one eye, both the result of childhood spinal meningitis. By the time she died she had gone completely deaf and was fighting off macular degeneration. Now, *that* is suffering!

    In my seventies I am reasonably fine in that regard; I have no incipient deafness, cataracts or glaucoma. One day I noticed a dark spot in the vision of my right eye. Years ago I had a retina problem in that eye so I went to the eye doctor immediately. No problem, it is only a harmless "floater", that is, a spot that moves around with your eyeball like a dancer in a water ballet. It's off to the side so when I try to look at it, it moves out of my sight. Every now and then it scoots across my line of vision and distracts me. For the first few weeks I had it I swiped at it thinking it was a fly or gnat, drawing some concerned looks from the people around me. The ophthalmologist assured me it was nothing to worry about and that I would come to ignore it, even to forget it is there, but I haven't managed to do either. Now I see it has developed its very own constellation of tiny specks trapped in a viscous universe.

    Lest I give the wrong impression, I'm in pretty good shape for a man my age, even for a man twenty years younger. I exercise regularly, am not overweight, and have pretty good muscle tone. And, most important, I have a good head of thick, wavy hair, more salt than pepper but that's fine. Over the years I've been complimented on it by both men and women, but for different reasons. The women like the look, the men are envious of its existence. Personally, I don't feel compliments are appropriate; I didn't do anything to deserve this hair, I had nothing to do with selecting my genes. As one doctor told me, I did a great job of selecting my parents, both of whom left this earth with beautiful heads of hair. All I have to do is keep it washed and get it cut, but thank you anyway.

    Prescriptions, I have a few: I have mildly elevated blood pressure, slightly high cholesterol, modestly high triglycerides, a barely clinical hypothyroid condition, and a mild case of depression. That's five prescriptions. You would think I should be in assisted living but it's not that bad. Notice, every one of my "conditions" is mild to moderate. The prescriptions have built up slowly over the years, one here, one there. Of course, like everyone else over fifty these days, I take a bushel full of supplements. When my friend and I meet for breakfast every couple of weeks we compare notes. In addition to the usual prescriptions he takes ginkgo biloba for his brain, thousands of milligrams of krill oil for his cholesterol, saw palmetto for his

Clueless In Paradise

prostate, and glucosamine with chondroitin and MSG for his joints. I feel pretty good about the fact that I don't need ginkgo biloba, at least I don't think I do. And since I no longer have a prostate gland due to a bout with prostate cancer some years ago, I don't need saw palmetto. I guess relentless optimists would call this a "silver lining".

Symmetry fascinates and amuses me, so it is with a certain amount of guilty pleasure that I can now report there is a lump of some sort on my left foot. It is the size of a garbanzo bean, just behind the knuckle of my big toe. I only noticed it recently and attribute it to the shoes I wear for tennis. They are of good quality and a brand I've worn with complete satisfaction over the years. The left shoe rubs against the affected area until I begin to play at which time it seems to go away but more likely goes unnoticed. A short visit with the doctor resulted in a referral to a podiatrist, who said it is not a lump or cyst but a bone. My big toe has a slight downward bend, what they call a "hammer toe, caused by the way I walk. (See "Footsies, pg. 117 for the grisly details.)

There is one thing that really bothers me: I have a heart that occasionally goes off kilter and speeds up for a while. It's a condition the doctors call tachycardia. When it happens, it leaves me a bit woozy, especially if it happens when I'm playing tennis or otherwise exerting myself. When it began doing this it scared the hell out of me and it still makes me uncomfortable as I sit there wondering if "the big one" is on the way. Almost as worrisome is the way the people around me react. The guys I play tennis with have become accustomed to my sudden trips to the bench where I sit while I try to breathe evenly and wait out the episode. When they first saw me do this they were understandably concerned. Heart abnormalities are serious matters for people my age.

My mates offered various suggestions and remedies: "take deep breaths", "should we call 911?" "Do you get many of these?", "Have you been to the doctor?" It took a few times for them to learn that talking makes it worse, so now they mostly leave me alone. One of them, a Taiwanese gentleman, comes over and administers acupressure on my palm, rubbing the "heart" spot. It doesn't help but I don't want to seem unappreciative so I let him hold my hand. After ten minutes or so I'm fine and can continue to play. In fact, I'm better than fine, I'm refreshed. I liken it to a car engine that gets clogged with fuel and needs to be blown out. Once that cloud of black exhaust comes out, it runs like a top.

My cardiologist says they're like hiccups. "Don't worry about it", he says. Why should he worry, it's not his heart hiccupping. Neither he nor my other doctors have any advice so I'm trying this and that. Deep breathing doesn't work; controlling my biorhythms doesn't work; I can't even *find* my biorhythms. I suspected for a while it had something to do with playing tennis on cold days, wearing warm-ups then taking them off when I get hot. I think I get them more often when I'm bending a lot. But sometimes I get them when I'm sitting down reading a book, or lying in bed going to sleep. I've tried adjusting my medications: nothing. So now I've cut out caffeine. I already drink decaf coffee, so I've eliminated my daily diet coke from Burger King. I love fountain drinks but what the hell, since I quit smoking years ago, cut down on eggs and red meat for my cholesterol, alcohol for my liver, and anger for my sanity, so why not my last guilty pleasure.

But I'm not bitter. I want to be healthy for as long as I'm here. If I make it to a ripe old age as my parents did, I'm going to be the meanest cuss in the nursing home. I'll be there grumbling under my breath with ringing ears, spots floating around in my eyes, my heart fluttering like a wounded bird, and giving everyone the stink eye. I'm reasonably certain that by then it will be my last remaining pleasure.

Herbert J. Moriarity

He called one night and told me he had a few sports blooper videos he wanted me to have. I knew he was facing surgery the next day to have his carotid artery cleared. The doctor told him it was not exactly routine but not all that unusual either so we weren't unduly concerned. I had no particular interest in the videos but I knew they meant something to him and so I thanked him while telling him I hoped this wasn't an indication he thought he wouldn't make it through the surgery. He said he just wanted to make sure I knew they were mine if something happened.

    Next day my wife called me at work to tell me Uncle Johnny had suffered a massive stroke while on the table. He was holding on but was in critical condition. By the time we went to see him that evening he was hooked up to monitors and not aware of our presence. The doctors said a fragment of the blockage material broke off and travelled to his brain. He was not in immediate danger of dying but was in serious condition. A television was placed over his bed with a note attached that read: "Patient loves sports. Keep TV tuned to sports events."

    My uncle John was born Herbert J. Moriarity in Brooklyn, N.Y. I have only sketchy information about his family but this much I do know: His mother died when he was quite young and his father, after a period of struggle as a single parent of , I think, two boys, threw in the towel and took young John to a

Clueless In Paradise

Christian Brothers orphanage. I never learned what happened to his sibling or siblings, probably because he himself never knew.

    Life in the orphanage was not easy. The Christian Brothers were strict and followed the teaching methods of the times, that is, young boys must be disciplined to tame their natural wildness and, in the process, the fear of the Lord must be driven into them. Johnny was naturally rebellious and had a hair-trigger Irish temper so felt the wrath of the good Fathers more than a few times. He told me that for serious offenses, such as getting into fights (once while playing second base in a game, the runner plowed into him. He yanked the base out of the ground and beat the punk with it) or for running away, which he did a couple of times, he was stripped naked and blasted with a fire hose.

    His father visited him irregularly and they would play catch outside. Eventually, the visits came farther and farther apart until one day they ceased. My uncle never volunteered information about his family beyond this; it was a time forgotten, not a part of his adult life.

When Johnny was eighteen, he ran away for the last time. He was of the age of majority and the orphanage had no interest in tracking him down. He was on his own. He spent time hanging out on the street corners of New York City with the other ne'er-do wells, getting into and out of trouble and learning to get by in any way he could. Eventually, he ended up in Rochester, N.Y. where he got a job as a dishwasher in a downtown department store cafe.

    Mary LaFranca, my mother's younger sister, worked as a counter waitress for the same cafe. Johnny was smitten on sight and proceeded to woo her with all the charm he could muster. He was rough hewn and could be volatile but Mary was born to a Sicilian family where she lived with her two sisters and two brothers; she was accustomed to volatile people. Still, this was a touchy situation. No one in her extended family had yet entertained the notion of bringing a non-Sicilian, a *straniero*, home.

Nature took its course and John Moriarity became my uncle. The family had reservations given his background and lack of prospects but somehow, it worked out. He won their hearts and he thrived in the warmth of a family environment. They went on to share many years of marriage before Mary passed away from cancer in her early Fifties. She was plagued by poor health caused by childhood rheumatic fever and debilitating migraine headaches in her adult years. Her family always blamed the headaches on the earlier illness and blamed the brain cancer on the headaches.

Uncle John became my best friend, took me everywhere with him from the time I was a child until I was married and raising my own family. Whatever else was going on in my life, I could always count on this man-child to come to the rescue. My father worked very hard to make ends meet and was not athletically inclined. He had been raised by a stern old world father which left little time for frivolous play. My uncle was a union painter who made pretty good wages and loved nothing more than to spend it on his wife and on us kids.

My parents understood and never expressed resentment at his ability to take me fishing, to ballgames, or anything else he had a notion to do. I came to realize that just as I loved his companionship, he loved having me to share his activities. I had my first ever cafe hamburger with him, one of many over the years. He followed the same ritual each time: he would

Clueless In Paradise

take the bun off and say, "you need an act of congress to find "boiger". He mispronounced many of the Italian foods we ate, much to the delight of the family. Thus, the delicious pastry known as canoli, became *cornerlis*. I fished my first rivers and lakes with him, caught my first perch and sunfish with him, and learned that coffee was the most important beverage on earth. Of course, he always wrinkled his nose at the first sip he took of any coffee he had not brewed himself. Then he'd down it and ask for another "cup of mud". Fact is, he did make a good cuppa mud.

My uncle stabilized a week or so after the surgery and stroke. He was still in very serious condition but had re-gained consciousness and recognized his family. Little by little he improved to the point where he could communicate with a crooked smile or wink and he regained a bit of mobility in his fingers. He even began playfully grabbing my wife's finger when she wasn't expecting it. His old playfulness seemed to return. When I visited, there was always some sort of sports event on the TV. We would watch a meaningless college basketball game in black and white and he would show distain for missed shots by wagging his head and making a *phfft* sound.

One day while sitting at his bedside watching hockey, it occurred to me just how many firsts I had experienced with this character. Besides my first hamburger, he took me to my first baseball game. I was so young that when he told me our minor league Rochester Red Wings were playing the Newark Bears, I got all excited and asked why there were no bears on the field. He took me fishing for the first time; on a Thanksgiving Day, he took me to my first ever football game featuring St. Thomas Aquinas High, our legendary high school team. He took me to see the Rochester Royals pro basketball team. (They later moved to Cincinnati and then to Minneapolis and changed their name to the Lakers.) And he took me to my first traveling roadside show, an event that remained a secret between us.

    He and my aunt moved to Southern California a couple of years after our family did. He took me to see the L.A. Rams play the Chicago Bears, my first pro football game. While we were out one day, he pulled into the vast, empty parking lot of the Santa Anita racetrack, stopped his '54 Ford Ranchero and told me to drive. I was fifteen and he thought it was time I learned. Aunt Mary looked very uncomfortable but knew better than try to dissuade him. So, I drove for the first time.

We watched the game with the sound down low. I spoke little because it was difficult for him to respond and it frustrated the hell out of him. A soft knock announced the arrival of the nurse, a stunning Jamaican lady. "Hi, Johnny" she sang. "time for your sponge bath!" I glanced at my uncle and he had the trace of a wicked little grin on his face. "Well, Unc, I'd better be going. You have a nice sponge bath." We locked eyes in what had to pass for complicity.

    A week later Terri and I went to the local mountains for an art show she was in. We stopped on the way out to say hi to him, then headed out. When we got back Sunday evening we received a call from my mother. Uncle Johnny had suffered another, more massive stroke, and died. Two days before the funeral service his wife, Margaret, called and asked me to eulogize him. She said he was such a good man and he deserved to be spoken about. I was, at first, frightened at the idea of doing it but I could not refuse her request. I too felt he deserved at least that much.

He had spent his childhood in a loveless, stressful environment bereft of family warmth and support. He could have grown to become a bitter, violent man but instead became a loving man of boundless generosity.

It was my first ever eulogy and I felt it went well. I said he was never as comfortable around adults as he was with the young. I related a few events from my childhood which illustrated how he had enhanced my life and that of my sister and cousins. At some things, they laughed, at some things they cried.

BATHROOMS
Or, The Groom of the Stool

Stop me if you've heard this:

A journalist interviewed a hundred and seven year old man reputed to be the oldest person alive at the time. He found him sitting outside his mobile home smoking a pipe and sipping from a glass of what appeared to be tea but gave off fumes of a much more substantial beverage.
 During the course of the interview the journalist asked the man, who had seen many changes, inventions and global upheavals in his long life, what, of all the things he'd seen did he find the most amazing. He pointed out to the centenarian that he was old enough to have seen the birth of manned flight, the introduction of the radio and television, two World Wars, astounding medical advances, and had even seen men fly into space and walk on the moon. The old gentleman set down his pipe and took a long draught of his drink and gave his answer directly, as though he had given the question a great deal of thought over the years.
 "Well", he said, "I'd have to say that what amazes me the most is the thermos bottle."
The journalist was taken aback by this answer.
"The thermos bottle! Really?" "Of all the amazing things you've seen, the thermos bottle amazes you the most? Why?"
"Well, you see", he said, if you put something cold in it, it keeps it cold. And if you put something hot in it, it keeps it

hot."
"Yes?" the journalist replied.
"Well", said the old fellow, "how does it know?"

    Of the many wonders wrought by man, the homeliest are often the greatest, although, often overlooked. Such a wonder is the flush toilet. Ask anyone who studies ancient societies or contemporary third-world societies and they will tell you that the presence, or absence, of sanitation facilities and effective sewage are defining factors in the overall health and well-being of the people who live there. And, perhaps just as important as its aid to hygiene is its ability to dispose of the incriminating evidence of our mortality.
    I know that I am ever grateful for and even awed by my toilet. Such a simple but ingenious design, such a critical yet relatively trouble free and remarkably unassuming device. Much like its close cousins, the faucet and shower, it provides more comfort for less cost than anything else in the home. But think of the last time you toured a prospective house or apartment with a thought to purchasing or signing a lease. I'll bet you didn't take a good look at the toilet or ask how the sewage system performed. No, you probably became enamored of the brick fireplace or the tile floors, or the track lighting, none of which will matter once you move in unless a commode is installed in the family room.
    By now, it is accepted lore that the flush toilet was invented by one Thomas Crapper, a 19th Century business man/inventor. According to sources I've consulted, it turns out that Mr. Crapper held a number of plumbing related patents for such things as drain improvements, pipe joints and manhole covers. The "Silent Valveless Water Preventer"

was an invention that allowed a toilet to flush efficiently. The British Patent for this product was issued to a Mr. Albert Giblin in 1898. Giblin worked for Crapper in his plumbing store and it is thought Crapper bought the patent from his employee and proceeded to market it himself. This may explain why he, Crapper, is the man associated with this most humble throne of kings and commoners alike. That, and of course, his auspicious cognomen.

    I grew up an urban urchin. My family restricted outdoors activities to hunting and fishing in locations that allowed me to return home the same day. The girl I married came from a California family that prized camping out. I assumed that I should enjoy camping with my wife and children. Turns out that whatever influence her family exerted on her in this direction failed to take. The first time we tried it was a disaster and the primary reason was the fact that our daughter was being toilet trained and the outdoor toilet was in an inconvenient location, that is, about fifty yards and three campsites away. Terri made numerous nighttime trips with her to the outhouse but she became upset and failed to perform each time.

    Next morning we pulled up stakes and headed home with equal amounts of relief and guilt. Later attempts to camp only reinforced our opinion. There were various causes, such as watching a six foot rattlesnake, fat around as a bologna loaf, leisurely cross the road near the entrance to our planned campsite. We once staked our tent over rocks that I swore were not there when we set up. There was cold, heat, unruly or inconsiderate campers who arrived in the middle of the night or who stayed up to all hours carousing. But mostly, it was the lack of comfortable bathroom accommodations that soured the experience. (I once dropped my toothbrush into the community toilet bowl on the first of a three night stay.)

No thank you. It has always been a dream of mine to have a sumptuous bathroom, one with a walk-in tub, water jets, multiple shower heads.... Like that. These things are costly and certainly represent a luxury, so lo these many years later despite a recent re-modeling project, we still have a small one with a standard tub that holds only enough water to cover parts of you, fewer and fewer parts of you as you become more substantial. On the rare occasions I bother to draw one, (another dream of mine is to have a man-servant to do that for me), I spend more time changing my position to maximize coverage than I do luxuriating in the experience.

I am not a tall or unusually large man, yet when I scoot down to submerge my upper body I have to bring up my knees. In doing so, the water rises up behind me and spills over onto the floor. I'm forced to form an embankment of toweling around the base of the tub for this reason. My wife does not find amusing the use of multiple towels for one bath.

Speaking of toilets, as I was, did you know that King Henry VIII and his father, King Henry VII before him, had among their retinues someone designated "Groom of the Stool"? The Groom of the Stool was part of the Royal Privy Chamber, a collection of "favored" men and women whose duties included all matters personal to the royal person. None as personal as the duties assigned to the Groom of the Stool whose duties are made clear by his very specific title. I, who can't stand to have anyone within twenty feet of the bathroom door when I'm therein, have no need for assistance or companionship. (My kids knew better than to travel down the hall past the bathroom when I was busy in there, although, they did take delight in sneaking up to the door and then telling me about it later.)

And, while I'm on the subject, allow me to voice a concern shared by many other men. What the hell's the deal with urinals and troughs?

Oh, the indignities of standing in front of one, especially the latter, alongside a collection of beer drinking sports fans. I only have sketchy evidence, including a lifetime of close observation, to disprove the generally accepted notion that the male of the species is less modest than the female, but speaking for myself and for other men I've known, this is not the case. And further observation indicates that the modern version of the female of the species is less modest than their mothers and grandmothers. Of course, physical arrangements do require different preparation and performance in order to successfully accomplish the mission, so some consideration is warranted. I'm not saying women should join us at the trough only that we should be extended a modicum of privacy for the sake of decency.

And, by the way, hanging newspapers on the wall so the urinal user has something to occupy them while taking care of business is not fooling anyone. Yesterdays sports page is of little interest to me. I refuse to make believe I'm reading about Tuesday's game when it's clearly Wednesday.

Good grief, would it kill them to build semi stalls at the urinals? I'm not suggesting that we have all cubicles as in the women's' room; I would like to get back to my seat before the inning is over.

Footsies

I don't like feet. Of all the appendages we civilized people expose without fear of arrest, our feet are the least appealing. Often, they are appalling as well. I see beautiful women whose beauty ends at their ankles: bony, splayed, little-piggie toes like Vienna sausages, disfigured by bunions and other signs of shoe damage, tiny, toenails so deeply imbedded they are only visible when painted a gaudy red or purple, and are set off by a toe ring on one or more of them, often on the long one beside the big toe. I don't mean to pick on women, but they are the sex most likely to expose their toes without the slightest twinge of self-consciousness.

    Most men have disgusting feet by default, although some aren't too bad. In fact, I've always been told my feet are not bad at all. I have my mother's feet and hands, a blessing if there ever was one. If you knew my father, you would understand. His feet were small, size seven as I recall. They suited him well since he was only in the neighborhood of five-six. He had fallen arches which he blamed on his years of having to jump down from the cab when he drove truck. Bunions, which may have looked average on larger feet, resembled dinner rolls on his. They caused his big toes to bend inward adding to the general disfigurement. His poor shoes were forced to accommodate his feet and so, bulged out on both sides. He was able to walk with certain jauntiness despite these maladies. But I do remember him complaining about how much his feet hurt.

    Growing up, painful feet and cruel footwear were commonplace among the adults I knew. Besides bunions and fallen arches, almost all of my relatives had corns, ingrown toenails or foot odor that could empty a room. The only time I saw anyone barefoot was when they were at the beach or lying in bed. My mother turned ashen one day we saw two children standing barefoot at a bus stop in the middle of winter. Their mother was with them but she was shod. The only explanation mom could come up with was they must be visiting hillbillies. Later, when we moved to Southern California, it became a common sight and she was forced to adjust, although she never countenanced it for her children. "I don't want you going around looking like Okies." In her defense, she did keep us from ruining our feet. her only concession was to allow me a pair of "sneakers every summer.

    Although their mother and father have good feet, both of my children have problems. My son supinates and has feet flat as crepes; when you do the wet foot test his print is completely absent the least hint of curvature in the arch area. My daughter has great arches but pronates worse than anyone I know. She can bend and misshape a new pair of shoes in a very short time. The soles of her shoes should be on the outer sides. And now, we see our grandson has his father's feet. Our granddaughter seems to have escaped the curse. So, imagine my chagrin when I learned recently that not only is my gait flawed, but my feet are damaged as well.

Clueless In Paradise

About two years ago I suffered a very painful nerve pinch near one of my cervical vertebra and went to the doctor. He referred me to a physical therapist who set me up with various exercises intended to improve my skeletal arrangement and to improve flexibility. While there, she asked to see me walk. "Walk away from me," she said. "Ha", I thought... piece of cake here. I walk well, I don't pronate or supinate and I have good arches. A pair of shoes last longer than the styles " After I had taken a short walk, she pointed out that I swing my right foot out before bringing it down in front of me. She said I don't push off with my foot so much as pull it forward. At first I couldn't believe it, but after watching myself carefully I realized she was correct. One of the exercises I left there with was one to help me walk more efficiently.

Flash forward a year and a half. I noticed a growth or protuberance on the top of my left foot, just behind the joint in my big toe. It was hard and fixed in place. I first thought it was the beginning of bunion, or corn. But it didn't hurt like a corn and it wasn't where a bunion would form. I thought it could be a cyst and even considered hitting it with a flat board the way some people do, hoping it would deflate and go away. I did feel it when I played tennis, probably because it rubbed against my tennis shoe.

Eventually, I gave up and went to the doctor. The doctor couldn't be sure what it was so referred me to a podiatrist. "Are there still such things as podiatrists these days" I asked? I hadn't heard mention of them since I was a kid, along with proctologists whom I hope are no longer around and if so, that I never have to see one. He was amused and assured me that podiatrists are in fact very much around and specifically for matters such as mine.

The doctor I visited worked out of a humble little facility not far from a strip mall. He was very personable and, more importantly, prompt. I had taken the precaution of washing my feet before the appointment but even so, I expected him to wear sanitary gloves. I mean, I sure as hell wouldn't want to spend the day handling people's bare feet with my bare hands. But no, he examined my foot *au naturel*. After a few moments of touching and pressing, he informed me that what I had was not a cyst or a corn but a protruding bone. He asked me to walk away from him. This time I knew about my swinging right foot so I tried very hard to walk correctly. I was about ten feet down the hall when I heard him say: "Hmm, very interesting. You have an unusual way of bringing your right leg out when you step forward which creates what we call a non-propulsive step. You should practice pushing off from the front of your foot when it is behind you."

"But, I've been walking this way for over seventy years," I complained. "A little late to be changing my walk, don't you think?

"Maybe so," he said, "but you should try. Now, here's what caused the up-thrust bone", he continued. "You have what we call "hammer toe" and it has caused the bone to push back against the bone behind it with the result that it has moved upward to accommodate the cramped space."

"I have what?"

"Hammer toe," he said.

I asked how that could be since my feet look perfectly fine.

Clueless In Paradise

He explained that my big toes are not flat to the floor but arched up a bit causing the misalignment problem.

"I can't believe it. I've know people with hammer toes and their feet are bunched up and cause them considerable pain."

"Yours aren't that bad," he said, "and since you are not feeling much discomfort and considering your age I doubt you want me to correct it surgically. But you should get better tennis shoes."

By the way, I thought later, why is this my fault? Why are these people telling me that my problem is due to the way I walk? Do you know how you walk? We all have distinctive strides. When my friend and I were in Air Force basic training many years ago, we found ourselves housed on opposite ends of the base. When we were both scheduled for base liberty, we'd talk by phone and establish a meeting place. The base swarmed with off-duty airmen wearing the same light military tan uniforms and yet we could each spot one another from quite a distance just by the way we walked. If I change now and we're ever in a similar situation, he might not know it's me.

I went out to buy a new pair of tennis shoes. (I recalled a time a few years ago when I was buying a pair of casual shoes and remarked to the clerk that the pair I wanted seemed too narrow even though they were the size I usually wear. His response was that when we get older our feet spread. I suggested he never go into the diplomatic corps.) While I was trying the tennis shoes out I mentioned my gait issue to the sales clerk. He said he had noticed that too! Now I imagine people walking behind me and saying,

"Linda, look at the way that guy walks. His right foot is non-propulsive!"

"Poor guy, Linda replies, "I wonder if he knows he suffers from Hammer Toe Syndrome or, "HTS".

If you suffer from moderate to severe HTS, Hammer Toe Syndrome, why go another day feeling uncomfortable in your shoes? Why wonder if people are talking about your gait behind your back?
    You no longer have to feel ashamed to take off your shoes in public. A simple adjustment to the bones in your foot by one of our trained specialists and you will be bouncing around like a youngster in no time. Only one treatment is required.
    Call our toll free number now to schedule an appointment and we will include a top quality aluminum cane in your choice of candy apple red or natural metallic finish as long as supplies last.

Don't wait! Operators are standing by now to take your call.

Gift Wrapped With Love

If we are defined by what we cannot do rather than by what we can, I wonder what it says about me that I am criminally inept at wrapping gifts. I mean, it's beyond all-thumbs. The mere touch of wrapping paper turns my fingers, not the most obliging digits to begin with, into anarchists. I may as well be working with soup spoons.

My ability to judge the length of paper I need to cover the box would be enhanced by blindness, at least then I could disengage my trembling brain and go by instinct. I'm either left with a piece too small or one large enough to wrap the kitchen table. In the first case I throw a tizzy fit, crumple it into a ball and throw it into the trash with all the force I can muster. In the latter case, I'm left trimming off an expanse of excess with at least a 75% chance of ending up with a piece of paper approximate in size to the one I just crumpled up and threw away!

Why do I continue to do this to myself year after year? I do it for love, why else? Over the years I've become at least a little better at it. I tell my wife that she is to consider my efforts to produce decently wrapped packages a labor of love; she should understand that compared to the gift itself, which any monkey with a credit card can purchase, the labor and heartache I endure to produce these pathetic results are equivalent to the effort that rich guy put into the Taj Mahal. James Joyce only had to write Ulysses. Hand these guys a roll of tape that has an irresistible urge to return to the spool the moment you think you're about to tear it free, or a piece of clothing that grows bulkier the more you stuff it into a box, and let's see how well they do.

This year, it was suggested that I just put the presents into gift bags. These are similar to shopping bags but are decorative and therefore suitable for the purpose. All you have to do is find a bag large enough or small enough for the gift and drop it in. Well, not exactly. You have to wrap the item in some sort of tissue paper to hide it from view or there is no element of surprise. Seems simple enough, but let's remember that we're talking about me here.

The first article I picked up was large, too large for the bag I selected. My legendary impatience, aided and abetted by my spatial dyslexia, contributed to my failure to recognize the problem until I had managed to tear the bag. Sweat broke out on my forehead and my language took a turn for the worse. I managed to find a larger bag whose width could accommodate the box which seemed to have doubled in size since being removed from the store. It wasn't deep enough but at this point I didn't really care. I stuck a bow on top and put it aside. The other two gifts were smaller and fit into bags more easily but it was here that I ran into the problem of covering them with tissue paper. It had to be done in such a way as to conceal the contents and make a nice "finished" look, then link the handles of the bags together with some sort of curly ribbon. These are small things and a normal person might just sigh and move on, but to me it was another straw on the bale already bowing the camel's back.

It all began when I was in kindergarten. Teacher had us make paper chains for Mothers' Day. We've all done this: take a

Clueless In Paradise

strip of colored construction paper, apply a glob of white paste, take the next strip of paper, loop it into the first loop, and like that until you have a colorful chain which you take home and present to your mom who, because she is your mom and only because she is your mom, loves it. As I recall, we had a few days to work on our project so there was no need to hurry, and teacher was there to assist us if we ran into trouble. Within a few minutes I felt something building within me that I now recognize as volcanic frustration. It was followed by self doubt and disgust. Once it struck, I was hopeless.

My otherwise perfectly good mind and assembled talents were nowhere in evidence. I cut and pasted and the paper twisted and popped open and the paste was all over my hands and face and hair. By day two it was obvious to the teacher that this young boy was not going to produce a suitable Mothers' Day chain. She salvaged what she could and let me take it home. Mom said she loved it, of course, but the die was cast; I was not cut out to cut and paste.

Now, honestly, what else is gift wrapping if not a cut and paste job? So, here I was, again, for the umpteenth time in my life face to face with my bête noire, my bogyman, my Cyclops, my Gordian knot. I kept telling myself that this bag thing was so much easier than cutting wrapping paper to fit a box and then having to tape the seam and corners so that it looked even and had no bare midriff or exposed corners. Just wrap the damn thing in tissue paper, apply the ribbon, scrape the tape off your fingers and go take a shower; you're beginning to offend.

After I tore the first sheet of tissue paper I managed to make the next one work. When I had both gifts properly camouflaged within their respective gift bags, I proceeded to select stick-on bows that matched the bags, (I'm not without a certain sense of style), and found a spool of ribbon. I'm sure you are familiar with stick-on bows, they have that rectangle of heavy paper on the back that you peel off to expose the adhesive. That is, unless they've been used before. (I don't know about yours, but in our family these things are re-cycled, and re-re-cycled.) This requires one to fashion a sort of ad hoc sticker sort of thingy by taking a piece of scotch tape and folding it back on itself to create a, yep, loop, which then can be stuck to to the paper portion of the bow and applied to the box or bag. The first time I pulled off a length of tape it popped out of my fingers and shot back to its home base where it immediately disappeared. For the next few minutes I tried over and over to find that damned tape end. Once I recaptured the tape, I applied to the bow, attached the bow to the bag and took my hand away. The cursed bag came with me. I attempted to detach the sticky strip from my finger only to find it stuck on my thumb, and so on, until I had spent what was left of my patience and tolerance. If you shake your hand real hard you will free yourself from the bag only to find that the bag has given up a sizable piece of itself in the process!

    Finally, It was all over. I took a break to mop my brow and do some deep breathing to bring my heart arrhythmia under control, I managed the final task with ease. One thing I do reasonably well is curl ribbon with a scissors blade. I put the gifts away, returned the implements of torture to their resting place and retreated to my recliner with an undeserved sense of accomplishment.

The great, ancient poet, I.M. Anonymous, wrote:

I found a stock-dove's nest,

Clueless In Paradise

    And thou shalt have yt,
The cheese-cake , in my chest,
    For thee I save yt.
I will give thee rush-rings,
    Key-knobs and cushings,
Pence, purse, and other things,
    Bells, beads and bracelets,
My shepe-hook, and my dog,
    My bottell, and my bag

Take them all with my limitless love, but please don't ask me to wrap them.

PART TWO

POISON

The first time was in the 8th grade at a junior high school. I was thirteen and our family had just moved to Southern California from New York State, so I was the new kid in class. I had spent the summer in the community before school started so I already knew what an "Okie" or an "Arkie" was: someone whose family had moved to California during the dustbowl years. So, I knew the boy next to me was one or the other. After some gettin' to know ya small talk, he popped this one on me:

"So, he says, "are you a nigra?".

I didn't get angry or feel insulted because I could see the utter innocence in his blue-eyed, freckled face. I was almost amused by what I considered his ignorance. With a good-natured grin I asked him what would cause him to ask me such a question.

"Well, cause you're all dark and such."
"No, actually. I'm Italian... never seen one?"
"No, the only dark folks I know are either Mexicans or nigras,"
"Well, now you've seen an Italian."

Later that same year it happened again. My closest new friend,

Sam Culotta

Back East, people knew an Italian from an African American or a Puerto Rican. From that moment on I knew I'd entered a different world.

Frankie, lived a little ways down the street. I was at his house often. His mother was always doing chores and his father, apparently out of work, looked old enough to be my grandfather. He always sat at their round dining room table which was covered with horse racing sheets and had a smoldering cigarette stuck between his yellow-brown fingers. His unkempt hair was the color of dirty ivory, He seldom looked up, seldom spoke, but seemed innocent enough.

On this particular day, Frankie was alone and he invited me into his special hangout: a small room in the corner of the garage where he kept treasures like the grainy black and white pictures of naked women he had stolen from his older brother. After a while a young lady showed up. She was a sort of girl friend/pal of his, and horse play ensued, nothing bad, just horse play. Suddenly, the door flew open and there stood his old man. He was short, bent, nicotine stained and looked righteous as a drunk tent revival preacher.

"What are doing out here, you little bastard?", he shouted at his son.
"You little whore!", he directed at the girl.
"And you," he said to me, "you little nigger, get the hell out of here!"

I got the hell out of there.

Eight years later:

Clueless In Paradise

The civilian guy kept trying to catch my eye from his seat at the bar. I suspected he had no good thing on his mind and as if to verify my suspicions he followed me down the hall when I left to use the men's room.

"Hey, coon," he croaked, "where you goin? Wait up." There was only the restroom and a closed door at the end of the hall. He was blocking the only way back to the bar. I turned to confront him and at that moment he threw a wild right that I saw coming but didn't quite avoid. His knuckle grazed my cheekbone and I felt a cut open. His follow-through drove his fist into the wall behind my head. A combination of fear and anger took hold of me and I swung. My lucky punch caught him on the side of the neck and must have done something to his Adam's apple because his beer-soaked eyes bulged and he collapsed forward a bit choking and grabbing at his throat with his good hand. I tasted blood, both figuratively and literally. Taking advantage of his minor collapse I swung my knee up under his jaw and heard his teeth snap together. The momentum of the blow sent him stumbling backward. The drunk bastard hit his head against the opposite wall and began to slide to the floor gasping for breath.

"You dumb son-of-a-bitch!" I yelled. "Haven't you ever seen a dark person who wasn't a negro, you stupid shit?" and began kicking him in the ribs. The feeling was overwhelming; every blow I struck stoked my anger and I felt myself losing control. I'd put up with crap like him many times over the years and always avoided responding. This was exhilarating, liberating and I had every intention of beating him to death.

My friend had gotten up and followed the guy when he trailed me into the hallway. Now he wrapped his arms around me from behind and shouted in my ear to stop. He pulled me toward the door at the end of the hall which turned out to be unlocked and led into an alleyway. By now I had regained my senses and we got out of there before we had to face the AP's.

None of this happened, of course. At least, not the fight. I don't expect my readers to be as neurotic as I am but I'm sure some of you have had one or more of those times when you were humiliated or angered but did not take action and only later fantasized over what you should have done at the time. Here's how it really happened.:

My buddy and I had come into downtown Spokane from the Air Base and were sitting in a beer bar sharing a pitcher. It was the early Sixties. Just a couple of guys in civvies having a good time. I happened to catch the eye of a man at the bar looking our way and knew immediately he was trouble. A few minutes later the waiter came to our table with two glasses of beer and told us they were from the man at the bar. We looked and saw him smile and give us a wave. Maybe he could tell we were Airmen even though out of uniform, so we waved back and thanked him.

"That's cool", my buddy said, "why do you think he did that?"

"I don't know, but he's been looking over here with a dumb grin on his face for a while so think he's up to something."

As we sat there drinking, another round arrived, then another. Now we had three beers each backed up and we weren't planning to stay there all night. A while later he climbed off his barstool and walked carefully toward the hall that led to the restrooms. He looked to be in his late thirties, medium build, thinning hair, but not a slob. Probably some repressed accountant out for a lonely evening on the town. Chances are he'd pick up a hooker later. He stopped at our table and, in the nicest way possible, asked me if I was a

Clueless In Paradise

nigger. My friend and I both laughed. "Nope, I'm Italian"
On his way back from the restroom he stopped again, this time he leaned down to me and repeated the question: "C'mon, man. You can tell me. You're a nigger, ain't ya?"

    I laughed him off again and he returned to his barstool, but by now I felt very uneasy about the situation. It was clear the guy was trying to get me to either verify his suspicions , or to tell him off. Either way, I figured he wanted to fight. My buddy was enjoying the beers and wasn't concerned. "He's a jerk man, but the beers keep coming." he said. A short time later, I saw him get up and leave. He must have tired of trying to get me to play his game.

We had a few rounds still backed up so we stayed until they were finished. He wasn't outside waiting. We had a good laugh over it all the way back to the barracks.

Groupings

The six of us were gathered together. We have known one another since our youth and have all celebrated our Golden Anniversaries.. We lived some distance from each other so this was no longer a common occurrence. When we were young we often spent our time listening to music, dancing, drinking and carrying on until we dropped. Sometimes we went away to mountain cabins, beaches and campsites. Today we hang out in our homes, in family rooms and living rooms, and on patios sitting within feet of a spa that has lost all of its once considerable charm. No one dares get into a bathing suit, and few of us still find pleasure in the discomforts of camping out.

Our views of the world, politics and religion, have changed dramatically since the early years but our personalities remain about the same. The men have become politicized, the women have become "religionized" except for my wife who hasn't become either and one of the men who has become both. Not surprisingly, conversation is constrained by these differences yet we manage to have a good time. What strikes me as odd is the lack of reminiscence. None of us is prone to re-live the "good old days". I wonder if this is common among old friends who gather only occasionally. We can't discuss domestic or foreign events for obvious reasons, so what do we talk about? We discuss health issues.

One is having heart problems: one is suffering the early

Clueless In Paradise

signs of dementia: most have high blood pressure and/or high cholesterol, or joints that have been, or need to be, replaced. Eye problems are common; we all wear glasses, some have cataracts, one has macular degeneration, and one or more have eye floaters. Declining hairlines are in evidence as are bald spots and thinning. These problems are not terribly serious but they do occupy much of our time and attention, which qualifies them as topics of discussion.

    We laugh about all of this. There is a certain comfort in sharing physical and mental deterioration with people you care about, people you can count on to give a damn. Discussing our health problems is a way to transform our personal decline into a communal one. Singular decline is tragic; communal decline is comic, or at least can be laughed at more easily. It may be a form of "whistling past the graveyard".

    Suddenly, one of the ladies asked if anyone has considered cremation. We were all raised in strict Catholic homes and spent at least some of our time in Catholic schools during a time when cremation was strictly forbidden, so the question sent shockwaves through the group. Not that most of us still consider it to be wrong as much as it just isn't a topic we've ever discussed. Nor do we generally chat about ever more evident mortality. One of ladies said, No! Others weren't sure what to say. How about you? I was asked. Frankly, I don't care what they do with me when I'm dead. Funerals are for the living and I want my family to do whatever pleases them: burial, funeral pyre, open air burial, New Orleans style, trash compacter, gunny sack, hefty bag; whatever they decide is fine with me.++ Then I told them I had written my eulogy to make things simpler for everyone. Here it is:

Sam Culotta

Eulogy

I would like it said
When I lay dead
(don't take too long;
you know how words
unsaid are quickly gone.)

I would like it said:
He was fair of heart
And middling in head
Not sharp as a dart
But fortuitously wed.

Put on his stone:
"He doesn't lie here"
Then pour me some scotch
before you head home.

I'll be waiting just there
In my LazyBoy chair
With my pants undone
And weeds in my hair.

I won't mind if you take
Fun from my wake
share stories about
My most grievous mistakes.

Make fun of the wrong turns I took
Like my silly attempts to write my own books,
that all of my songs were half-baked

Clueless In Paradise

Take your best shots, go ahead,
Then dim the lights and put me to bed.

I don't really expect this to be read at my funeral...but, maybe at my "after party". It could happen. I mean the opening few lines are meant to be more than humorous. What people wish for in life doesn't often happen, let alone in the afterlife. My mother always told me she wanted the Ave Maria sung at her funeral; that was her only request. I told her it would be done as she asked. When she died I went into a music site and downloaded both it and the iconic Italian song "Mama" The latter was my idea because of the song's remarkable beauty and tenderness. I played the CD on my computer and on my stereo system to make sure I had recorded the songs correctly. Beautiful; not only would Mom be pleased but there wouldn't be a dry eye in the house, which would please her even more. On the way to the funeral, I played the CD again on my car stereo. Beautiful! When we arrived at the mortuary I gave the CD to the facilitator with instructions for when to play each recording. She assured me she would do as I requested.

When the moment arrived for the Ave Maria to be played, nothing happened. The facilitator came down the side aisle and whispered into my ear that the CD would not play on their music system. She was genuinely sorry and very apologetic but there was nothing to be done. My mother's sole request went unanswered. But the food, catered by a fine Italian restaurant, was very good and the guests seemed to enjoy themselves.

Postscript: Our friend who raised the question of cremation was only with us a few more years. She passed away suddenly, tragically, after a brief illness. She and my wife were life-long friends. In keeping with her wishes, her remains were cremated.

Et Tu, Santa?

"All children have to be deceived if they are to grow up without trauma."
—Kazuo Ishiguro, *Never Let Me Go*

It began when I figured out my father was putting the coins under my pillow after I lost a tooth. This meant there was no Tooth Fairy. Soon after that, bang! The Easter Bunny was dead. Out of desperation I held on to Santa Claus despite copious evidence that the fat, jolly guy was just another broken promise, but eventually even my still unformed intellect felt insulted and I was forced to capitulate. This was the last straw, or so I thought.

One day a friend told me that his father and mother "did it" and that's how he was born. A few heartbeats passed before the import of what he said hit me right square in the brain. Oh, my God! If his parents did it, then mine did too! Not *my* mom, no way! My dad, well, maybe, but not my mom! I couldn't look at either of them for a while. "What's wrong honey?" mom asked, "You look sick. Do you feel alright? Come here. Do you have a fever?" She felt my head and assured herself I was fever free but she still had a worried look on her face. With a herculean effort I managed to convince her I was just thinking about stuff; nothing was wrong with me. Since I was known to be moody and sometimes lost in thought, she just gave me a hug and went on about her business. It took a while longer before I was able to accept the fact of my parents' veniality but I got past it eventually.

At school one day Sister asked me and another student to go to the drug store for her. We were in the 5th grade so we didn't have to be asked twice. The druggist found her order, took the money and sent us off with a small paper bag. It wasn't long before curiosity got the better of us and we sneaked a peek to see what drugs she had bought. It was a bottle of pills to treat constipation! Well, we couldn't believe it! Constipation? We never imagined that nuns even went to the bathroom let alone became constipated. We suddenly possessed information worth a king's ransom but realized also that if we told our buddies, word would get back to Sister and there would be holy hell to pay. So, we vowed to keep it a secret between the two of us. I tell you, knowing that a person relieves themselves the same as everyone else is powerful stuff. Sister lost a whole lot of her mystique that day.

So, to recap: In just a couple of years I learned there was no Tooth Fairy, no Santa Claus, and no Easter Bunny. I learned that my father did unspeakable things to my mother that resulted in my being born, and that even "Christ's bridesmaids" were subject to the same excretory inconveniences as the rest of God's children. My innocence was gone, my eyes were opened; this had to be as bad as it got. It was not.

I came face to face with the fact of my mortality when I was nine or ten years old. Just like my grandfather and our friends' son who drowned during swim team practice, I was going to die. How could this be? How does any sane person recover from such a brutal realization? Why are we brought into being just to be snuffed out some day in the future?

Clueless In Paradise

I suddenly appreciated the concepts of God and heaven. I wouldn't die after all! I would shake off this mortal coil and my soul would ascend into heaven where I would be with God and his angels and saints. My soul would skip among the wispy clouds humming along with the choir of angels for all eternity. I could not really get my head around eternity, but I knew it was a long, long time. Besides, the people whose wakes and funerals my parents dragged me to,(in retrospect, more often than normal), featured old Italian *comadres, compadres* and assorted *paisans*, no one I knew. This helped implant the notion that I probably was not going to die regardless of what my parents told me.

Recently, we had a death in the family. Our kids consoled our grandchildren in the traditional way; they explained that their grandmother was now in heaven and was happily looking down upon them. What's a parent to do? The truth would either be beyond the kids' understanding, or if not, would traumatize them. So, we fib....again. The children were five and six at the time, so events washed right over them and life continued without a ripple. Then one day, our grandson went to his parents in tears. He sobbed and sobbed and finally managed to babble what was torturing his innocent little mind. "I don't want to die and go to heaven because I'll have to leave all my toys here!" After assuring him that he wasn't going to die, he stopped crying and went back to play.

Actually, he had hit the nail on the head in a way only a child can. If we were so hot about reaching our heavenly reward we would volunteer to be next, but we don't want to leave all our toys behind either. I know a few people who are unbothered by the fact of their eventual demise, or they have managed to convince themselves they are. These people just don't think about it. They say, "Why do you think about depressing things like that?" I say, it's because I'm cursed with an appreciation of reality, and I ask why they *don't* think about things like that. They say, because it's depressing, so why think about it? I remind them: "You are going to die, you know." And they usually say something like: "Stop it! Let's talk about something more cheerful!" To which, I say: "OK, Santa Claus will be coming soon, have you baked cookies for him yet?"

Live every day as though it's your last, they tell me. If I thought each day was my last I don't think I'd be in the mood for a party. I often think of the condemned who are offered their choice of anything they want for their last meal. One poor guy in Arkansas ordered a feast of fried chicken and fixin's followed up with pie. When he couldn't eat all the pie he asked the guards who came for him to keep it for him, he'd eat it later. If they didn't know it before, that should have been proof enough they were about to execute a man who didn't quite understand the implications of what was awaiting him. In a civilized world his death sentence would have been commuted right then and there.

What normal person is hungry at a time like that? If I was going to be executed later in the evening, I'd have no appetite at all, sorry. I guess I'd ask for a couple of anti-depressants washed down with a fifth of my favorite scotch followed by an expensive cigar. I'd rather go to the death chamber with a stogie between my teeth, laughing uncontrollably, but they don't allow a "dead man walking" to smoke on the way to the death chamber. Why the hell not? Are they concerned about his health? Second hand smoke issues? Go figure. Anyway, with my luck, I'd get sick, throw up and be stone sober by the time the priest asked me which scripture reading

Clueless In Paradise

I'd like him to intone on our way down the hall. Now there's a choice I hope I never have to make, but off-hand, I'd prefer Molly Bloom's soliloquy.

Interesting how little these lies we tell bother us, in fact, we don't even consider them lies. We say we're only allowing innocent children to enjoy the magic that adults invented for them for as long as they can. We know that one day they will fix us with that knowing smile and we'll be busted. That's only if we're lucky. I've known kids who were inconsolable when they learned the truth. A family friend told me she finally conceded defeat late in her youth but then, when she was twelve, she happened to see Santa climbing into a car outside a department store and lapsed into belief.

Eventually, all kids accept the fact that the things they most enjoy about Christmas and Easter are not real. But the reality soon,(often immediately), gives way to the thought: who cares? We still get cool stuff at Christmas and lots of chocolate at Easter. Sure, we don't get squat for losing teeth anymore, but that one wasn't all that great to begin with and most of our baby teeth are gone anyway. Some day when they're grown and have children of their own, they'll be able to enjoy it all through the eyes of the kids. Santa will make a comeback followed by the bunny and fairy and all will be as it should be, again.

Look At It This Way

In which your fearless author dares tread where wiser men won't.

From the moment you were conceived, you began to age. You will never be younger than at that instant of conception. The long or short trip to the end of life had begun. And what are your primary, perhaps only, biological duties? They are to stay alive and to reproduce, the latter of which may be viewed as an extension of the former. It is another way of saying: see to the care and feeding of your genes so you can pass them along thereby achieving a sort of immortality. A *sort* of immortality, because you and your genes are subject to the whims of your progeny. Of course, there are other ways to deal with the immortality problem: art and faith, for two. I'll get back to you on these but for now let's just stay with the material world.

I'm not a trained, or even untrained, philosopher, but if I was, I'd posit that the will to live, or "the survival instinct", trumps all other matters of human and non-human existence. Trite idea, you might say. You may be right, but one thing I've learned on my longish journey through life is that the most obvious truths are often overlooked or ignored. We humans like to place ourselves above the other life forms on earth because, well, because we're self-serving egotists, (which is another way of saying survivalists), by nature. The lowly amoeba is a single-celled organism with no sophisticated organs, a rudimentary nervous system and a very limited world view. It exists to exist. It eats by surrounding microscopic food with empty chambers called vacuoles and absorbing them into its system, a very simple system that absorbs nutrients and supplies enough energy to enable them to blob around. But this shapeless organism manages to reproduce, and with great efficiency.

We learned in grammar school biology how they do this. An amoeba's nucleus contains the essential materials that make it an amoeba and at some point something called binary fission begins. The nucleus begins to stretch apart and eventually splits into two. This is considered asexual reproduction because amoebae are sexless. If they were not, this could be considered either a prototypical form of self love, or the first known incidence of incest. These "daughter cells" are identical so amoebae can be said to be inbreeding like crazy, but it doesn't seem to produce less viable offspring because they thrive quite well.

One more thing about amoebae. They are reactive to stimuli. Our biology teacher told us that if you shine a beam of light through a container of swimming amoebae, they will react strongly to that light when they wander into it. And when the same ones near the light beam a second or third time, they opt to retreat from it. That's evidence of a surprising ability to learn from experience and adjust to their environment. I'm not proud of this, but I established the "Amoeba Standard" for my children. If they did the same silly or disobedient thing more than twice I bestowed upon them the "Amoeba Award". It was accompanied by my pronouncement that "even an amoeba can learn to avoid trouble! What is your problem?" I suppose this seems cruel to today's parents, but at least I didn't force them to wear dunce caps.

Sam Culotta

The lowly protozoan manages to survive and reproduce itself with remarkable efficiency. Our complex process of attraction, courting and mating seem like overkill by comparison. We humans have the advantage of well developed brains which enable us to use reason. We like to think we also have cultivated tastes which allow us to make intelligent choices when seeking to mate. We know also that many times choice is a luxury we cannot afford. But seriously, our goal is the same whether or not we acknowledge the fact. When push comes to shove, so to speak, we are just carrying out our genetic imperative to reproduce ourselves. Coupling up and producing young do not, however, answer our need for individual survival.

It's great that we are able to pass on our genes but that doesn't relieve our desire to take care of "number one". We want to live, and once we have others in our family group we feel obliged to keep them alive even if only to satisfy our physical and psychic needs. I'm not convinced our prehistoric ancestors experienced altruism; incidents of genuine altruism are rare even in our enlightened times. It would be many centuries until Thomas Hobbes wrote his "Leviathan" (1651) and Rousseau, his "Social Contract", (1762). Both attempted to establish a political/social order in which man gives up some rights to a Sovereign or a government in order to gain protection from what Hobbes termed, "the war of all against all" as exists in nature.

Uncivilized, brutish men had to hunt, kill and fight to maintain a household. If the neighboring cave man took a fancy to your lady there was no divorce court; there were stone axes. To minimize the risk of being relieved of your mate, or your head, you might team up with that neighbor and learn to share a kill and to protect one another against attack by "outsiders". Enough of this sort of behavior led to formation of larger groups of cooperative humans and eventually tribes, which then became organized well enough to develop patriotic zeal and to wage wars.

Tribalism remains the essential social structure of human society. Over the ages man has subsumed it into his daily life often without being aware of it. Our tribe, or family, or group, or state or country are held dear to us and any threats to their purity are considered threats. This can be as simple as resentment toward a different ethnic or religious group moving into our community; it can be based on racism, bias, prejudice or any fear of "the other".

What is ours is to be protected from the influence of people unlike us. Various social experiments have been conducted over the years in which students are divided into groups of different hair colors or eye colors and told that one or the other is the superior group. In short order, resentment and prejudice arise. These groups behave like tribes at the slightest indication of being better or worse than those outside their tribe.

The current anti-immigration mood in America and some European nations is only the latest in a series. In our country it began as soon as white, Christian Europeans became the most powerful citizens of the New World. Until then, white people were the immigrants and intruders, feared and reviled as savages by the native peoples who then became reviled as savages in turn. Of course at some much earlier time they themselves played the role of conquerors after which they formed tribes and began warring with one another. I maintain that this aggressive behavior is the manifestation of the basic will to survive. Social Psychologists offer various examples of this phenomenon even going so far as to suggest that infidelity in both men and women is a subconscious effort to spread one's genes beyond the restraints imposed by monogamy. I doubt anyone has managed to use this as a defense in divorce court.

So, our genes are passed along via reproduction and this promises at least a physical means of existing after our lives end. But really, is anyone comforted all that much by the notion that our progeny will carry on with our DNA? I don't know anyone who finds this the solution to their fear of death. Our literature and art are filled with the anguish of knowing we are mortal creatures with limited life spans. Here's a cheery tidbit from William Butler Yeats' famous poem, "Sailing to Byzantium":

"Consume my heart away; sick with desire and fastened to a dying animal"

Yeats, the grandson of a devout Rector of the Church of England was himself a member of the Church of Ireland. He later became involved in magic and occultism and spent his life conflicted over these different belief systems. How do we face the knowledge of our mortality, this angst, this feeling of hopelessness, this fear? Yeats, for one, faced it with creativity, for to create is to defy death, not to ignore it or overcome it but to put on a brave face as if to say: "take that, Death!".

We write or paint or sculpt or compose music for various reasons. In my case, writing brings me pleasure and a sense of self-worth. I can convince myself that I'm doing something worthwhile and that someone somewhere will appreciate what I do. Whether or not my work will provide me some sort of continuance after my death is not that important to me. Art may also function as a personal signature or self-portrait.

Clueless In Paradise

The great works left by the masters and revered to this day have the power to keep their creators ever alive in our consciousness. When we look at Michelangelo's statue of David or De Vinci's painting of the Mona Lisa, or listen to a Mozart concerto, to name a few obvious examples, we can't help but to associate these amazing works with their creators.

But, art can be more; it can be material evidence of a spiritual system such as that of the ancient Egyptians who believed in the immortality of their bodies and spirits. They perfected ways to preserve the bodies of the dead by mummifying them and left ample evidence of their intent by placing them in great tombs with water and food for their posthumous journeys. The art that covered the walls of their tombs reflected a style that was not changed over the centuries in order to maintain the uniformity of the ideal man or woman. Most modern artists have a less spiritual goal in mind but must share some hope of being remembered. Unless your name is Woody Allen.

"I don't want to achieve immortality through my work; I want to achieve immortality through not dying. I don't want to live on in the hearts of my countrymen; I want to live on in my apartment."

Allen was born into a Jewish/American family but would never be confused with a person of faith. His statement, however, does betray a fear of the inevitable and an awareness of mortality similar to that of Yeats. Allen uses humor to make life bearable. We all have our ways of dealing with the problem; I'm glad he has chosen to make me laugh.

Because we are the only animals who have knowledge of our existence, we are the only ones faced with the awful awareness of our mortality. Ancient people turned to nature for comfort or to make sense of existence. They needed plants and animals for food, clothing and shelter. It was a simple step from that to assigning supernatural powers to natural phenomena. If it didn't rain enough the crops died and they starved. If they couldn't find game they starved and went without clothing. How better to explain natural disasters like drought, flood, wind storms, thunder and lightning than that they or someone else had angered one god or another. Rituals were devised to appease the gods, often including animal and human sacrifice. The Incas raided neighboring tribes and brought their captives home to be slaughtered in colorful ceremonies. The blood of their victims was offered to the gods in an attempt to placate them.

 Later civilizations, often called "advanced", moved beyond this blind, ritualistic means of surviving the unknown and indefinable. At some point we humans came to the realization that we are special, by God, and as such we must be the product of a force greater than us, greater than all. There are differing opinions as to how this came about. Atheists and others will say that humans created God in our own likeness. Defining human-like deities gave us a much better sense of controlling our destinies than having to make nice to gods in trees, mountains and rivers. People of faith have various creation scenarios with a full inventory of prophets, angels and saints.

 There are many estimates of the number of religions being practiced in the world today. I'm not inclined to get into the various sources of this information but one of them, The World Christian Encyclopedia, comes up with 19 "major world religions" and 270 "large religious groups" including Christianity which is estimated to contain 34,000 Christian groups

Clueless In Paradise

worldwide. "Over half of them are independent churches that are not interested in linking up with the big denominations."

One thing you can be sure of is that every one of these thousands of religions and sects are certain *they* and they *alone* are the *true* faith, with a special conduit to the Divine. That fact in itself is not surprising or troubling, but what is troubling are the numbers of religions who go a step further by declaring believers of other faiths misguided or, in some cases, evil. The number of people killed in conflicts directly or indirectly associated with religious differences is horrific. Nations, taking their lead from tribes are able to convince themselves that theirs is a country blessed by God and therefore superior to other nations.

A few decades ago, a fellow by the name of Hitler promoted such an idea. In Paul Reid's "Preamble" to the final volume of "The Last Lion", William Manchester's great biography of Winston Churchill, he quotes Churchill saying over lunch one day: "Every nation invents God in its own image." It came across as a "supreme blasphemy", yet Reid goes on to point out that, "even Hitler claimed that God was on his side." It is important to note that England held the same opinion of their own country during the years of their great empire.

Once again, tribalism is front and center. In order to be "special" others must be less important, often to the extent of being less than human and as such not worthy of existing. The holocaust is the most tragic example we have in our lifetimes. And it took generations to end the bloody conflict between Catholics and Protestants in Ireland's "Troubles". Today, as I write this, Muslims, Christians and Jews are killing each other throughout the Middle East and parts of Africa. Islamist terrorists ravaged Paris, France, just a few days ago, killing 129 and injuring many others. The attack was planned and carried out by members of Islamic State in Syria, ISIS, or Islamic State in the Levant, ISIL, if you prefer. Their stated mission was to kill Christians in retaliation for Christians killing Muslims. France, Russia and the United States are currently bombing ISIS strongholds, in retaliation for Muslims killing Christians. And so it goes.

    We are most comfortable among our own, people who share our interests, our faith, our politics, ideals and even our skin colors and ethnic identity. I was born in Rochester, New York and lived there until I was thirteen when my family moved across the country to live in the suburbs of Los Angeles, California. As long as they lived, my parents never forgot their Rochester roots. We had numerous visitors from "back east" and every time the conversation turned to the city of our birth: old haunts, old favorites no longer there, this or that part of town no longer what it was, everyone moved out to the suburbs so the inner city is like a ghetto now... etc. And great "discussions" about what street was just off some other street or on which street some business or other was. I could see the delight in their faces as they talked about these things. I know they loved living in California and never regretted moving us out here, but neither did they quite get over the loss of their native ground.

    When my wife and I visited Rochester in 1998, it had been over forty years since I had been there, but I felt completely and comfortably "at home" at once. Everywhere, there were people who looked Italian and had familiar surnames. When we went to the cemetery to visit the graves of my maternal grandparents there were numerous headstones bearing the names of aunts, uncles and cousins. I was back among my "people", my tribe. I felt in touch with my past and I felt a sense of continuity that somehow reassured me about the future. It was a feeling I had not realized was missing in my life those forty years. It may be attributed to having grown older by then, since we tend to look backwards with longing as we age.

In 2007 our first grandchild was born and I was moved to write "Family Suite" a memoir/family history of mine and my wife's families. In it, I made clear that my humble effort was only a starting point, a touchstone for anyone from a succeeding generation who may want to continue from where I left off. I suppose I'm guilty of wanting to be remembered but I'm realistic enough to understand that a book can resonate for years or, like an echo, simply fade away.

I will close with one more quote.

"One might accept death reasoningly,(sic), with every aspect of the conscious mind, but the body was a brute beast that knew nothing of reason."

Isaac Asimov, *Pebble in the Sky*

John Cameron Swayze's Camel News Caravan

"A fifteen minute news show. Swayze always wore a flower in his lapel"

I still see that small screen television with the black and white images of Swayze reporting on the progress of the Korean War, about the presidential candidates and the complexion of the presidential race. And he still had time to "hopscotch" the world for headlines, all in fifteen minutes.. The dapper little man with the flower in his lapel signed off with, "That's the story, folks—glad we could get together. And now, this is John Cameron Swayze saying good night." And millions of Americans reached for a Camel.

Those were the days of Camel, Lucky Strike, Pall Mall, Chesterfield and Phillip Morris. There were other brands but these five are iconic. The Camel's pack back then had its famous camel image on the front and the image of exotic Turkish buildings on the back. We had a stupid joke. We'd show someone the front of the pack and ask: If you were stranded in the desert, where would you find shelter? The clever answer was: why just go around to the hotel on the back.

Lucky Strike had that big red bull's eye on the front of the pack. It was simple but effective. No frills cigarettes and proud of it. The Lucky's pack was just the right size to fit in the rolled up sleeve of your tee shirt, just make sure the front was facing out so the red spot could be seen through the material.

Clueless In Paradise

Lucky's claim to fame was that the tobacco leaf was toasted which made for a light smoke. So right here you had the demarcation between it and Camels; the latter was made from Turkish tobaccos which offered a richer, more robust flavor. Just as there were Ford and Chevy guys, there were Camel and Lucky guys. Believe me, it mattered. The Lucky joke involved their advertising gimmick, "L.S.M.F.T.: "Lucky Strike Means Fine Tobacco". The wits of the day preferred" Loose Sweaters Mean Floppy Tits".

(Don't blame me; I'm just the reporter.)

Pall Mall came in a striking red pack befitting its royal blood lines. It was first produced in Britain in 1899, hence the fancy Art Nouveau lettering and great shield which featured a crown and two regal lions pawing at one another. The shield also contains the Latin script, *Per aspera ad Astra:* "Through {the} thorns to the stars". Below the shield is another Latin script, *In hoc signo vinces:* "By this sign shall you conquer". And just to insure that their brand would be recognized as the regal cigarette it was, it was longer than that of its competitors.

    Pall Mall became the first "king-size" cigarette. The aim of all this was to appeal to a better class of consumer, and eventually it worked. It became the best selling "ciggie" in the American market by 1960 and reigned until it was pushed out by Winston, ("Tastes good like a cigarette should."), in 1966. We cool kids liked the length of Pall Malls, but weren't moved to leave our Luckys or Camels. And besides, you couldn't carry a pack in the sleeve of your tee shirt. Chesterfield seemed to appeal more to mature, blue-collar smokers. It was certainly popular but I don't recall any of my friends smoking them unless they had copped them from their Dads. They came

Sam Culotta

in a pretty classy package which featured the name in script with a red column topped by a crown. It garnered fame in the Sixties when Ian Fleming revealed that Chesterfield was Bond, James Bond's, cigarette of choice. My father smoked them for a while, and if memory serves me, my first ever toke was off a burning Chesterfield butt tossed from a passing car and cadged by my cousin Sonny.

"Hey, you ever smoke?" "Nah", I said. (I was eleven, he was nine.)
"Here", he said. "Okay", I said.

    His little sister went straight upstairs and told my aunt Suzie who told my mother, who told my father. When we got home Dad called me to him and stood in the doorway with his arm up. This scenario always led to him ordering me to "get in this house" then he'd clout me in the back of the head when I passed under his arm. He said he knew I had smoked and that as punishment, he was going to make me smoke a whole pack until I threw up. When he saw the light shine in my eyes, he knew he had lost the battle and never followed through. He even left the doorway so I could enter safely.

Call for Phillip MMMMMooooorrrrr-rrrrrAAAAAiiiiisssss!!!!!" Anyone of a certain age will recognize this call as that of the cute hotel bell boy with the formal uniform and cocked pill box hat. He was a "little person" hired by Phillip Morris to be the symbol of their advertising campaign. To do justice to his history, I include an excerpt from the Wikipedia entry for Phillip Morris which relates the legend of how an advertising mogul by the name of Milton H. Biow discovered Johhny Roventini while working on an ad campaign for the cigarette

Clueless In Paradise

company. In those days, hotel lobbies were often elaborately furnished and used as meeting places. It was common for persons to seek one another out. As the story goes:

" Biow and Lyons (a business man) had apparently been unnoticed by the 22yr.old bellboy when, according to the legend, Biow approached him and paid Johhny a dollar to page a "Mr. Philip Morris" throughout the lobby. The small bellboy repeatedly cried out "call for Mr. Philip Morris" in his distinctive high pitched voice, several times, not knowing there was no such person. He did not realize he had been performing an audition.

'I went around the lobby yelling my head off,' Johnny recalled later, 'but Philip Morris didn't answer my call.' Roventini initially thought that his call had been both legitimate and unsuccessful. He was soon to learn that he had been wrong on both counts. He was later quoted in *Variety*: 'I had no idea that Phillip Morris was a cigarette'. Roventini, whose voice was reputed to produce a perfect B-flat tone when doing his call, went on to a long career representing Phillip Morris and achieving a great deal of personal fame in the process.

The cigarette came in a golden brown package with broken gold horizontal stripes. It also featured an ornate shield framed by, what else, the ubiquitous British lions. In the center of the shield were the letters, P.M. When I got a bit older, I became a Phillip Morris smoker, maybe because, like Chesterfield, some of our fathers smoked them. I had a friend whose high school aged sister was a closet smoker. He could steal two or three at will because even if she suspected him, she wouldn't dare squeal for fear of being discovered by her parents.

Kools, then, the only menthol cigarette, featured

Sam Culotta

a cork tip, precursor to the filter, but intended only to keep the smoker's lip from sticking to the paper. And you could still find Wings at cigarette counters. These were a popular smoke in Europe that hit the U.S. market in 1940, the year I was born. Originally produced as a low price alternative during the war, they were a rough smoke, even for the times. I tried them once or twice; they tore up my throat.

Raleigh cigarettes, like Kools, had cork tips but were usually shunned by any guy who had aspirations to be cool. To add to their market appeal, the packs, which sported the image of a dashing Sir Walter Raleigh, included coupons which could be redeemed for a range of goods, similar to those in the S & H Green Stamp catalogue. (Full disclosure: in my late teens I was a Raleigh smoker because my father and grandfather were smoking them and they wanted the coupons. Also, it was easier to bum one when I needed to.)

Grandpa was living with us in those days. He had a considerable hand tremor the doctors thought was Parkinson's disease, which he outgrew in his eighties. The tremor caused considerable problems for him when he smoked. I can close my eyes and see him as he extracted, lit and smoked his Raleigh cigarette. His hands were not ordinary hands: they were large, twisted by years of farming and by advancing arthritis. When he decided to smoke a cigarette he performed a series of actions. He reached into his shirt pocket and removed the pack. Next, he unfolded the foil over one half of the pack. He would poke around and carefully extracts a cigarette, a considerable feat for fingers better suited to pulling vegetables out by their roots. Daintily, while holding the cigarette in one hand, he would re-fold the foil and return the pack to his pocket. Now the cigarette must be prepared by tamping the tobacco down so that the cylinder is tight. This is a carryover from earlier times when smokes were often loosely packed; it was no longer necessary but don't tell grandpa that. He would hold the cigarette between the thumb and index finger and slam the side of his hand against the wooden arm of the chair. I had to stifle a laugh because the cigarette never actually touched the wood. The force of the blow would have smashed it if it did.

He was ready to light up now, a procedure which involved pre-moistening his lips by puckering twice and placing the prize in his toothless mouth with great care. Finally, he'd reach into his pocket for his matchbook, shakily peel off a match, crush it against the flint and pull it into flame, The violence of this act sent sparks flying which left tiny burn holes in most of his clothing and the upholstery of his chair. With great seriousness and attention, he guided the match toward the cigarette with his shaking hand. After a successful meeting of fire and tobacco, he'd take a long satisfactory drag, shake out the match, deposit it in the ashtray and resume his hooded-eyed boredom.

Give him credit. He quit when my parents convinced him he might burn down the house. He was in his early eighties by then and lived until he was ninety-eight, lending support to the claim that not smoking will extend one's life. My father was a man with remarkable will power. He prided himself on his ability to quit "whenever I feel like it", this despite having continued to smoke while he was recovering from a bleeding ulcer. He made good on his word in his mid-fifties; he just stopped one day and never took it up again. He never passed up the opportunity to trumpet his achievement when someone mentioned how difficult it was to break the habit. "Hell", he said, "When I decided to quit, I just stopped. Just like that! Never went back." If it worked for him, it should

Sam Culotta

work for you, dammit!

I smoked from that day my cousin picked up the burning butt when I was eleven, until I was forty-eight years old, albeit with a few aborted efforts to quit along the way. By then, I was addicted to menthols, usually Kools, sometimes Salems, but would smoke anything available when necessary. I also spent many happy hours with a pipe or cigar. I was convinced that pipe and cigar smoking were healthier so turned to them when I was trying to quit cigarettes. To this day I remember with great fondness the wonderful sensations of walking into a new tobacco shop to nose around their pipe tobaccos. I still have a collection of pipes in an attractive desk-top cabinet and will occasionally hold one in my teeth just for the hell of it.

My four years in the Air Force reinforced my habit. The military will do that to you with its long stretches of tedium interrupted by drinking bouts and carousing. In basic training it seemed everyone smoked. We were housed in old, highly flammable barracks with butt cans attached to posts. The Training Instructors (TI's) warned us about failing to douse our butts in the cans. They seemed to enjoy reminding us that the building we were living in could burn to the ground in mere minutes.

When we drilled, we were given smoke breaks during which everyone either took out a cigarette or begged one from the poor guy who happened to reveal a full pack. When we were finished, the TI ordered us to "field strip" our butts. This entailed taking the edge of the paper seam and stripping it down vertically thus allowing the butt to be opened and the tobacco to be scattered to the wind. The remaining tissue thin paper we rolled up into a tiny ball and secreted in our pockets. Our TI held filter-tipped cigarettes and their users in low regard. "And any of you pussies smoking filter tips, make sure

Clueless In Paradise

you put the Tampax in your pocket."

  I've had a couple of cigars over the years, most notably, one I smoked with my son after the birth of our first grandchild, but other than that I've remained chaste even though every time I'm going to Laughlin I swear to myself I will buy a big cigar and enjoy it immensely, which I never do.

If I said I never miss the comfort of reaching into in my shirt pocket for a cigarette, or packing a pipe with aromatic tobacco from a pouch, I'd be lying.

And that's the story folks - glad we could get together.

Teach A Man to Fish

Give a man a fish and he'll eat for a day. Teach a man to fish and he'll eat for a lifetime."

Like most ideological propaganda, this sounds good at first glance. Makes sense, doesn't it? Give them a fish (i.e. a handout, a free lunch, a leg up, a welfare check, etc.) and they will take it, use it and come back expecting more. Rather than teach then to rely on their own means we weaken them and ultimately reinforce their dependency. Yes, it makes sense, at first blush, but a closer examination reveals the flaws, flaws that are not accidental errors of logic but designed fallacies intended to gull those with established prejudices and those who lack the ability or interest to apply critical analysis to the matter. The statement derives its impact through the power of metaphor and so I will use the same method to examine it.

"Teach a person to fish." Who will teach a person to fish? You? Who will supply the fishing gear? Who will provide transportation to a location where fish may be found? Who will teach them how to clean and cook the fish? How about supplying them with a cooking device? And don't forget, lines get broken, hooks and lures get lost, so gear has to be re-supplied. And, by the way, since it's going to take time to transform these non-productive drains on society into productive ones, they just might starve to death in the process.

Clueless In Paradise

Is it alright if we give them a few fish to sustain them during the conversion process? Who's going to cover this? You? Or shall I, or we, the public, take on the expense and effort in order for your notion of how to make a person independent come to fruition? If we, the public do take on the expense and effort needed I assume you won't mind using our tax dollars to do so. After all, once the poor person is happily pulling fish from the lake and eating regularly they can earn money selling the excess product and become financially secure. Then they can pay taxes and become a contributor rather than a drain on the economy. If we don't use tax dollars it will have to come from the private sector. While we Americans are noted for our charitable ways, gathering money for the indigent is not high on the list of well-funded causes. I cannot envision a volunteer corps of concerned citizens willing to donate their time and treasure to this project. If such a corps was created it could well become hierarchical and begin to take on the characteristics of a government agency.

The following is an excerpt from a recent article in the Los Angeles Times.

"Los Angeles spends more than $100 million a year coping with homelessness including as much as $87 million that goes to arrests, skid row patrols and mental health interventions, according to report released Thursday {April 14,2015}."

The article goes on to discuss the growing problem and the ineffectual attempts by resource starved agencies to deal with it. Homeless encampments which are appearing in greater numbers are not only a blight on the city but are considered a safety threat to nearby residents. Efforts to establish safe, temporary housing meet with obstacles, among them the fact that residents are uncomfortable with neighbors who were previously living on the street. Among these justifiably upset citizens must be a number of folks who would nod their heads in agreement with the fish story above. Note that the majority of the expense is used to police and remove the homeless; very little is used to provide them aid, training and housing. The article further quotes retired UCLA professor, Gary Blasi, who has "studied homelessness extensively."

"It's a thoughtful and a positive step to look at resources the city already is spending that produces very little. People need to understand it is more humane and cost-effective to help people become not homeless."

 A case could be made that the professor is more concerned with giving a man a fish than with teaching him to fish. The comments could be perceived as "bleeding heart liberalism" by not showing enough concern for the failure of existing financial efforts to help the situation. But it is difficult to overlook the point being made by Blasi: that keeping people from being homeless must be a part of the solution. And thinking that this sort of "charity" should be left to churches and other organizations misses the point.
 I am reminded of the words of philosopher Isaiah Berlin who wrote, and I paraphrase: "there is not an answer to a serious problem, there are *answers*."(Emphasis mine.) If we assume that people at both ends of this discussion are well-meaning rather than ideologically driven, the problem of caring for people in need and of limiting the number who slip into that condition, the answers will include both giving the man or woman the fish and teaching them to fish. Those who deny that either one of these methods is palatable should

excuse themselves from the table.

My cousin, (let's call him Bill), is a middle-aged man approaching his sixties. He lives in Section 8 housing, a California state run program which subsidizes rents for those whose incomes are below the poverty level. He has lived in this housing since he was a teenager and his parents found themselves unable to sustain sufficient income to live otherwise. Bill's father was what we called "slow" many years ago and his mother was a submissive woman completely under his control. Bill suffered from childhood epilepsy and because of a lack of medical and social programs at the time, he was not given the sort of attention and specialized training he would get today. As a result of all this, he was declared "retarded" which is now termed "developmentally disabled". Despite this disability he proved to be a high-functioning teenager and was even able to find a job and purchase a small pick-up truck.

Being around him requires patience and understanding; he is functionally illiterate and given to bouts of childlike panic when upset. The fact that he has always been a very large person creates a sense of discomfort among those who work with him and around him. Eventually, he lost his job, lost his truck, and ended up non-productive and dependent on others.

Bill is now alone in the apartment, his father and my aunt having passed away in recent years. He is morbidly obese, has a heart condition and is almost crippled by a bad leg and knee. He is so large he cannot fit into a normal car or small truck. Unless he gets a ride from a friend with a large enough back seat he relies on a taxi service to get to appointments. His hygiene is so bad that the taxi drivers, who know him by now, spray the interior of the cab before and after his ride, a humiliation that even a developmentally disabled person can feel. He has a State designated care giver who helps to keep the apartment in order and run errands for him, a task she is not authorized to do. When my parents were alive they often gave him small amounts of money or dropped off food to supplement his diet. My wife and I have called upon the services of church and community food banks to help us help him.

Bill is one of many thousands who end up in similar conditions. If it were not for the Section 8 Housing program he would be either in a care home or nursing home or, worse. We know that it is only a matter of time before his health deteriorates to the point where he will have to leave his apartment. If Bill did not have the State program and relatives nearby to sustain his meager life-style, he might well be on the street asking for a handout and being looked down upon as a lazy slug unwilling to get up off his butt and do something about himself. Life for him might have been considerably better if he had been born twenty years later.

I hope the Bills of today make out better. I hope our society, which arcs slowly, often grudgingly, but inexorably toward caring for those less fortunate than us, will have worked out ways of dealing with the homeless and the indigent through means that both relieve their immediate needs and help them to improve their lives. Of course, there will always be a certain number of people like my cousin, who cannot be expected to do much to help themselves thus leaving them in the position of needing our help to survive.

We as a nation certainly have the resources and expertise to develop better solutions. We have to get over the notion that the filthy looking guy with the shopping basket outside

McDonald's with his hand out is someone who is unable or unwilling to make the right choices.

Our American ethos of self-reliance, for which we should be proud, and our unfortunate distaste for those who fail, often provide us an excuse to avoid the moral responsibilities that are a requirement of good citizenship. Those who tell us the fish story may be confusing human beings with the deer we are told to not feed in National Parks when they come to your car for food for fear of making them dependent on hand-outs.

Pity The Poor Pessimist

(Further musings on mortality)

"Death doesn't worry me that much, I'm not frightened about it...I just don't want to be there when it happens." Woody Allen

You realize how inconsequential you are when you return to your computer after an hour or so and find you have only one email, and that is an ad for "The Better Bra".. Not that I need something to confirm my lack of consequence. This may sound pessimistic. I'm always accused of being a pessimist when actually, I'm not worthy of pessimism. I am driven to be a realist and find that optimism is the greatest obstacle to that goal. It takes wisdom to avoid falling into the trap of optimism. Put another way, you must be either naïve or willfully ignorant to ignore life's daily disappointments. Pessimism is not exactly evidence of intelligence either, but at least its disappointments are more like good luck.
    I come from a long line of pessimists and malcontents. In fact, I'm hard pressed to think of an optimist in my father's family. My mother's family is sunnier by nature but I don't think any are actually optimists, just more hopeful than hopeless. My father believed he could cause people to die just by visiting them in the hospital. He also believed the Dodgers would lose if he went to the game so spent the baseball season

Clueless In Paradise

in his stifling hot, enclosed patio ear pasted to a small, lo-fi radio, fuming and crowing by turns. His brother, my Uncle Joe, turned against the Lakers and the otherwise much beloved playing legend and then, General Manager, Jerry West, because he believed West had the nerve to cut a player with an Italian surname.

My paternal grandfather, the family fount of all pessimism and negativity, spent his old age sitting in a chair mumbling against any and all who crossed his line of sight. Sometimes he did it when no one was around which leads me to believe he stored up insults both intended and unintended as a squirrel stores up nuts for the winter. The only thing that made him chuckle was the sight of people making asses of themselves. He got a huge kick out of watching people like Charlie Chaplin, Buster Keaton and especially Laurel and Hardy. Summers when I was out of school I would stay up late to watch the old movies with him. I'd like to say we bonded during those jumpy black and white late-nights, but I would be flattering myself.

With an outlook and reputation like mine, I should hesitate to express my thoughts about "The End". A few hours ago I was sitting in the waiting room of a medical facility awaiting my turn at an echocardiogram. Next to me was an elderly man who couldn't help talking to me even though I was intensely occupied with a game of four card, Spider Solitaire.

"What do you think about all the killing that's going on these days? Every time I turn on the TV it's bad news of some kind."

"Well, I said, "I guess there's always been a lot of this stuff going on but we just didn't hear about it every day."

"Yeah, that's true. It's just pretty depressing."

"Yes it is, but remember, none of us gets out of here alive."

He chuckled, told me he is eighty-four and then related the following:

"Damnedest thing. A younger friend of mine told me a while back that I needed to go to my reward, that I was using up *his* time. *Your* time? I told him it was my time and I intended to use all of it I can get. Know what happened?" (Of course I did, but I didn't have the heart to ruin his moment.) "He up and died two months later, and here I am!"

None of us gets out of here alive. Can you argue with that? No, you can't, but you might say it's unnecessary to point it out. We all understand we're going to die some day so why bring it up? What's the point? To which I say, hell, I don't know I just think it's a good idea to bring people back to earth when they're trying to understand matters of dire consequence in a simplistic way. How can I explain that we humans have been killing each other ever since there was someone else to kill. Am I being a traitor to my own race by pointing out that humans are animals like every other animal, just a bit more sophisticated?

I can hear some of you say, "But we have souls! We have reason! We can feel empathy and behave altruistically!" You may believe that, even I may believe that, but it doesn't really make much difference does it? The fact remains that no other species of animal kills its own kind for any reason beyond self survival and even then it is usually the outcome of instinctive conflict over territorial or mating rights. Well, a few animals are known to kill for the simple reason that they hate or

Clueless In Paradise

are jealous of another member of the species: that would be chimpanzees and some other great apes. Not coincidentally, these critters are the closest living relatives to homo sapiens.

But we are special. There was a time when to say a woman had maternal instincts seemed perfectly reasonable. Women do not have instincts. Animals have instincts. We humans are the only animals who can use reason, the only ones who understand we are all individuals and we all have free will. We are not driven by base instincts, in fact it is said we have learned to control our base instincts and in return have gained free will. We are capable of recognizing right from wrong and are charged with the responsibility to choose what is right and reject what is wrong.

Depending on your world view, something happened eons ago that triggered the "big bang" which got the whole thing rolling, or, about six thousand years ago a divine being, let's call him or her God, created mankind in his or her own image and started the whole thing rolling, or, something in between occurred; God created the universe and let nature take its course. Whichever of these happened, one fact is inescapable: from that very micro-second it's been downhill ever since.

Consider this: The universe could not possibly be any younger than it was at that magic moment. Science tells us that stars were formed by space matter drawn together by forces too complex to go into here, and that those stars attracted other space matter we call planets, asteroids, comets and such which make up galaxies such as our own Milky Way and solar systems such as our own. We know all this matter zips around in space, collides, creates other chunks of matter, gets fried in the heat of stars or otherwise decomposes. We know that stars with their unfathomable mass and heat destroy what comes too near and that things which drift too far away succumb to unimaginable cold. We know that lucky chunks like our own earth are right in a Goldilocks Zone thus are able to accommodate life forms. And we know that stars have a finite life-expectancy as well. Our very own sun, born over four and a half billion years ago, is middle aged and will one day compress into a mind-boggling mass of matter so dense it will suck the light out of itself and become a black hole. When this happens, earth and every living thing on it will die. Heck, every living thing on earth could die before the sun consumes itself if conditions become hostile to life due to atmospheric change or self-immolation.

    A great deal of controversy surrounds these facts. Many people argue that some are not facts at all. But I don't believe anyone in their right mind does not accept the basic outline of the universe's birth and eventual death. Where there was nothing, there will be nothing. Now, here's what gets difficult for us human animals to accept: we too will return to the nothingness from which we came. And this is where religion enters the picture.

    We're just too darn special to be like all the other plants, animals and minerals in the universe. How else explain this reasoning mind and feeling heart? How could someone as wonderful as you or I be nothing more than the product of a chance gathering of stardust with an ability to develop? The only explanation for such a phenomenon is the existence of a Divinity. Whether that Divinity resides in the trees, rivers and mountains, has multiple arms or multiple eyes or one eye in the middle of its head matters not at all. And all the better if it resembles us, or we it.

Clueless In Paradise

It may require that we kill something, someone or many someones to placate this Divinity's anger or jealousy. It may be benevolent or cruel, forgiving or vengeful; it may have all these qualities in its repertoire ready for use on demand. There are a few qualities it *must* have, for without them it would not be divine: it must be immortal, it must protect us from harm and, most importantly, it must offer us a share in its immortality. Immortality is what we seek; it is the ultimate solution to the problem of death. The problem of death is only a human one. No other living thing contemplates its eventual demise.

Young humans do not worry about it; they cannot grasp the concept. And when they are faced with it, they accept whatever explanation we adults give them and go right on with the business of being young. The time must arrive when they will have to come to grips with what Jean Paul Sarte termed "nausea" in his so named novel about a man dealing with the inescapable facts of his existence. Evidence is all around us. At some point we are forced to recognize there is no one in our grandparents' generation still living, then in our parents'. Then our peers begin to pass. If life were a baseball game, guess who would be in the on deck circle?

Religion is both the solution and the problem."People of faith", previously known as "believers", have the comfort of a promised afterlife spent in the bosom of the Lord. They also fear displeasing God and being condemned to burn in the unquenchable flames of hell for all eternity. People without faith miss the comfort of an eternal reward but avoid the terror of hell. Most people have a foot in each position. They cannot give up the idea of God and heaven but are not able to accept the idea of hell. There is also the variation made famous

Sam Culotta

by the 17th Century French mathematician, physicist and philosopher, Blaise Pascal. "Pascal's Wager" as it's known posits that humans all bet with their lives that God does not exist. Given the possibility that God actually does exist and assuming an infinite gain or loss associated with belief or unbelief in said God, (as represented by an eternity in heaven or hell), a rational person should live as though God exists and seek to believe in God. If God does not actually exist, such a person will have only a finite loss (some pleasures, luxury, etc.)

I relate most closely with Pascal's view of the problem. But I do have a problem with the idea of hell. I cannot conceive of a Divinity creating a flawed creature and allowing the poor thing to stumble through life only to end up in a place of eternal damnation. When challenged to explain my personal belief I answer by saying: "I hope like hell there's a heaven but know damn well there's no hell." And if neither of these is correct and there is no creator, no heaven, no hell... what is left? What is left is what was there before we got here.

Where were we before we were born? Were we spirits floating in the eternal ether waiting to be called forth to life? What does it matter if we were; we didn't know a thing about it, existentially speaking. And, if after we die we are nowhere again, or again an ethereal being, what of it? If you have ever undergone major surgery you will remember that one moment you were talking to the anesthetist, the next you were in a recovery room with a pleasant nurse telling you it was all over and your family are waiting to visit you. In the time you were "out" the surgeon opened your body cavity, delved into it, pushed organs and tissue aside, removed unwanted or unruly part and, finally, put you back together with staples so that you looked like a poorly sealed package ready for the UPS man.

Clueless In Paradise

Where were you? Maybe the same place you once were and will be again. I suggest that I am closer to being an optimist than I am to being a pessimist. What sort of pessimist would discount the existence of hell and look forward to either heaven or nothing at all? And wouldn't an optimist look at the specter of death fearlessly? Of course, an optimist might rather believe he or she is going to heaven while continuing to believe in hell since the existence of hell makes the thought of heaven that much more appealing. And what self-proclaimed optimist doesn't take some comfort in pitying pessimists their certain misery? Maybe I do optimism a disservice, if so I apologize. But no one apologizes to the poor pessimist.

Among The Humans

In the late Sixties and on into the early Eighties, I walked the streets of downtown Los Angeles to and from the buildings where I spent my days making money and not much else. I saw people there in various states of misery and euphoria. These were the days of tax revolt and budget cuts, psychiatric wards forced to shut down and disgorge the sick and troubled onto the city's streets. The idea was to medicate them. Of course, they had no support system, so ran out of medications or forgot to take them, or just didn't care. The streets became their homes and haunts.

The lady outside the Greyhound Bus Depot wore a long gossamer dress. She had stars painted on her face. The dress waved like seaweed around her ankles as she roller-skated in a large circle. Inside the circle a woman lay face down bouncing her forehead off the tiled walkway, crying hard. But nothing bothered the girl with the stars on her face and the moon in her eyes. She circled and sang no tune, with words only she understood.

In front of Clifton's Cafeteria on Broadway, preachers–in-training practiced their two- steps- and- a -foot-slap with their bibles in hand while their classmates and teacher stood against the wall to evaluate them. Across the street a sweet, cinnamon-brown woman in a white sarong and head scarf stood back from the corner and offered to anoint any and all saying: "Will you accept a drop of awl in the name of Jaysus?" Her angelic smile blessed every hand extended or withdrawn. I sometimes bought a kosher dog at the hot dog stand.

The owners, a man and his wife, had numbers tattooed on their forearms and could hardly keep up with demand. One day walking with my friend, Glen, who wore thick glasses, we met a man crossing the street. He looked at Glen and said: "You ain't kidding nobody. You got Jew eyes you Jew bastard." We laughed and kept going.

There was a man in leopard skin shorts and an athletic shirt who shadow- boxed beside you as you waited for the light; there was the famous character who showed up once on the front page of the L.A. Times. He wore a piece of paper in his hat band that said "Jesus Saves," who might come up behind you and shout "YOU'RE GONNA GO TO HELL!!!!" in your ear and scare the living shit out of you. One day I saw someone knock the poor old guy into oncoming traffic, but he wasn't hit. Doughboy was a dapper little black man who wore a crisp WW I uniform, puttees, hat and all, and held a cigar holder with a cigar stub stuck between his teeth. Everybody loved the Doughboy... he seemed the least likely person to cause trouble, but one day the police picked him up and threw him into the paddy wagon for some reason. When the cop closed the door and jumped into the driver's seat all hell broke loose inside and he had to dismount and beat the doors with his night-stick to stop the thumping that was going on. Doughboy must have sat next to the wrong guy.

I parked on the roof of the bus depot only a few blocks from skid row and walked up 6th Street to my office. One very cold winter there was a pathetic wretch who stood against the wall in tattered clothes, His feet were bare and oyster- blue. He hugged his torn shirt to his chest and begged from every person who passed by. I gave him money and tried to make eye contact with him but couldn't. A well-intentioned businessman gave him a pair of brogans for his blistered feet but he threw them into the street. He didn't want shoes, he wanted money to satisfy his need for wine. Sometime later he was picked up, cleaned up, and deposited back on the street to start again, fresh.

I spent many stolen moments in the L.A. City Library where I probably saw Charles Bukowski but wouldn't have known him from any other derelict. And on the street again I swear I saw Richard Ramirez. He walked down the street with a boom box on his shoulder blasting AC/DC, glaring, daring anyone to object. I didn't know at the time he was probably the serial killer we called The Night Stalker. All I knew was I didn't want to be anywhere near him.

Robert Blake drove by in a camera-mounted car filming Baretta. At Owl Drugs, I looked down on Paul Anka's bald spot as he bought three caramel swirled meerschaum pipes for Christmas gifts. "I saw you on Johnny's show the other night," the sales clerk said. I bought the last pipe for myself.

At lunch one day there was a big stir, so I took my food to a back table on the patio by the parking lot. The noise followed me and when I looked up, Telly Savalas was standing against the brick wall, ten feet away. A photographer began shooting as "Kojak", in a fitted sharkskin suit that accented his "package", went through a series of poses. James Cahn, his partner on the show, stood behind the photographer and tried to make him laugh. The onlookers envied my proximity; I only wanted to eat my lunch in peace and quiet.

The short guy sizing up the front of an old abandoned

Clueless In Paradise

firehouse with an eye piece was Ron Howard doing location research for what turned out to be "Backdraft." One of the two men walking in front of me in the jewelry district was veteran comic Jan Murray. Sweet Melissa Gilbert of "Little House on the Prairie" fame stood beside me at the crosswalk, all grown up. And on and on…. Stars were plentiful, but a peaceful lunch was precious.

    Later we moved to posh quarters in a high-rise further uptown. Nothing is as lonely as a high-rise building. I don't know why. I worked in them for years and stared out the window too much of the time. Lucky for me the German tourist who leaped from the top of our building one day bounced off another person's window on his way down to the street. It traumatized the lady in that office. When we left to go home he was still there in the middle of the intersection covered with a yellow blanket. Another day, a crew doing road work nearby managed to cut the power cable to our block and our staff had to walk down twenty three flights of stairs to get out. The ladies removed their high heels but some of them still ended up with trembling legs.

    There was a bad earthquake early one morning that trapped one of my staff, my secretary and me on the 23rd floor. My staff guy was only a few weeks back from a kidney transplant and needed medication. My secretary was seriously pregnant and scheduled for a caesarian. Long story short, we were assured we'd be among the first to be evacuated but they emptied out the upper floors beginning with the executive suites. When we got on the elevator hours later the security guy told us we were the last tenants remaining. So much for that captains and ships business.

    We had to wait to be rescued because we couldn't use the stairs. The staircases in our building were attached to the

Sam Culotta

walls and if one gave way it would collapse those beneath it like a house of cards. Each floor had a supply of body bags. They were parsed out based on the estimated population of that floor. Their existence provided no comfort to staff. If the power went off, as it did on more than one occasion, the air conditioning did as well. And, oh yes, the toilets gave up the ghost after the first and final flush.

Later, bank headquarters were moved to an even taller building, the tallest in the city. One of my carpool members worked on the executive floor, sixty stories up. On a windy day you could feel the building sway. On a clear day you could see the entire Los Angeles basin. It was quiet up there; executive secretaries walked on carpeted floors and most of the offices were empty since the executives were usually somewhere else doing whatever executives do. One visit was enough to last me a lifetime.

A lot has changed since I left downtown. The colorful folks are either gone or well-hidden. No more beautiful souls with starry faces or broken hearted ladies bouncing their heads off the sidewalk. I doubt either the Doughboy or the Jesus Saves preacher is still alive. I like to think the honey-voiced dispenser of holy "awl" is living out her days among others as spiritual as she. My friend Glen got drunk one night and drove off the road into a ditch, killing himself. I suppose the hotdog vendors with the tattooed forearms are retired now. I hope they did well and that their last days were a hell of a lot better than their first. I think of them often.

The library burned down and was rebuilt and incorporated into the very same tower that housed the bank. It's now called the Tower Library. And the bank has been taken over by another bank, which took over the bank I

Clueless In Paradise

worked for. Most of the people who walk around in suits are very young and walk fast while talking into cell phones or texting, or listening to music through ear buds. Almost no one meets your eye, and if someone does, you can bet they want something. I live in the suburbs and rarely have a need to go into the city these days. I don't miss the traffic but I do miss the energy.

People raised in suburban or rural environments are bothered by the bustle of city life; they tell you they can't imagine having to go there every day. But if you ask those of us who have spent a great deal of time in the midst of it all, we will tell you there is a hard to define serenity there. I think it is the comfort of anonymity. Jim Morrison of The Doors wrote: "People are strange when you're a stranger," but after a certain amount of time in their midst you're no longer a stranger and they're no longer strange, you're just anonymous, and there are worse things.

Authors Anonymous

Good afternoon, and welcome to Author's Anonymous, a program dedicated to bringing otherwise unknown or little known authors to the attention of our listeners. I'm your host, Radford Davies, and today's guest is Sam Culotta. Mr. Culotta is the author of "Sleeping With Lumbago", Often humorous, always personal, stories." published by Youwish Press. Sam Culotta lives here in the Los Angeles area with his wife of forty-nine years. He is also the author of "Family Suite" a memoir/family history of his and his wife's families. "Sleeping With Lumbago" was chosen from a number of authors' submissions.

RD. Mr. Culotta, welcome to Authors Anonymous. How are you today?

SC. I'm fine, thank you Radford.

RD. Please, call me Rad.

SC: Happy to be here, Rad.

RD. How about your back problem, the lumbago referred to in the book title? Has it gone away?

Clueless In Paradise

It went away and stayed away. All that medicine, all those treatments, and nothing worked better than waiting it out. Funny, huh?

RD. Yes. So, Mr. Culotta, let's discuss your book.

SC. Please, Rad, call me Sam.

RD. (Small chuckle) Very well, then... So Sam, let me begin with a question about the subtitle of your book. The cover reads "Often humorous, always personal stories" but the title page reads: "Often humorous, always personal essays." Which are they, and why does the title page differ from the cover?

SC. Good question, Rad. Truth is, it's both. The title I submitted read, personal essays, the title they put on the cover reads, personal stories. I consider it one of those *felix culpas*, or, happy mistakes. Many of the pieces, (notice how I cleverly avoid using either term), are personal stories but some, like The Chicken Came First, or Oh, Lucky Us, are clearly more on the order of essays.

RD. By your definition, what is the difference?

SC. Well, I guess I'd say that the stories are based on factual events and the essays are based on my opinions. Does that sound right to you?

RD. Yes, it does. Thank you for clearing that up.

SC. You're welcome.

RD. By the way, I really like your title. Our listeners should know that the title is drawn from a joke that appears in the last, ah, piece. But we'll get to that later.

SC. Why don't we just agree to call them all stories to save a lot of confusion?

RD. Good idea. Now, without getting into personal information about you, I think it's safe to say that most new authors are young people in their twenties or thirties.

SC. I was seventy-one when the book was published.

RD. Well, OK, I wasn't sure if you were sensitive about your age. Seventy-one is an unusual age for someone to produce their first commercial book.

SC. I am sensitive about a lot of things, a fact made evident in the book, but my age isn't one of them. In fact, that's why the short author's bio on the cover reveals that my stories cover seven decades of my life, and that I still live with my wife of forty-nine years. Too late to hide my age.

RD. Ha, Ha... yes I would have to agree.

I was amused by the Irvin S. Cobb quote that you included in your book. Let me read it: "A good storyteller is a person who has a good memory and hopes other people haven't." Are you a fan of Irvin Cobb's writing?

SC. No. I'm afraid I know next to nothing about him. I was

Clueless In Paradise

just thumbing through a book of quotes for something appropriate and thought: bingo! There it is!

RD. Ha, ha, I see. Well, it does fit the purpose doesn't it?

SC. Yes, it certainly does

RD. So, let's talk about these stories of yours. They cover episodes in your life over a period of seven decades, beginning in the forties and continuing through to the near present. So, is Cobb correct?

SC. Well, really, what's the difference? My memory is pretty good, almost scary at times, but more importantly, most of my friends and family have terrible memories. And the other people I mention are either dead or no longer correspond with me. Besides, we all know that writers have to take some liberties with the truth to give their memories flesh.

RD. True. Have you heard from readers who question or disagree with events as you describe them?

SC. That's a good question. I've heard from a number of readers, but they only have nice things to say. Some say it brings back memories of lost family members and events. Of course, these readers are all family and friends; some were given free copies so they really can't complain.

RD. Let me ask the obvious question. I'm sure there are other writers out there listening, and they wonder how sales of this sort of book are going?

Sam Culotta

SC. Sales? Well, let's just say that if this interview stimulates listeners to rush out and buy "Sleeping With Lumbago," there is a very good chance my sales could break two hundred by the end of the year.

RD. Two hundred? Well, let's hope your appearance here has the desired effect. Let's talk about some of these stories... let's begin at the beginning, because I found the first one captivating, humorous and certainly personal: all qualities that would make a person want to read on. "And Then There Were Two", recounts an embarrassing event that occurred at the Catholic school you attended. You were a youngster of ten or eleven?

SC. I'm not exactly sure, but I was definitely pre-pubescent.

RD. (Chuckle) Yes, I'd say that's definite. Anyway, without giving it away, let's say it was a surprise physical examination arranged by the school to give you and your classmates a cursory check up and to refer you to your family doctors if any problems were detected. Is that about right?

SC. Yep. Sister sprang it on us. Our parents hadn't been advised. We were just sent down the hall to a make-shift examination room.

RD. So, there was no permission slip authorizing the exams?

SC. That's right, no permission was asked and none was granted. Those were unenlightened days; schools had complete control, especially parochial schools.

Clueless In Paradise

RD. Very interesting. But there is much more to the story than the embarrassment of the exam itself isn't there?

SC. Oh, yes. But why don't you give me your thoughts on that.

RD. O.K., I will. There is an underlying tension concerning your relationship with the nun, and, judging from the second story, with nuns in general. I get the feeling that you resented their power over you and over your parents. Am I correct?

SC. Oh, hell yes, Rad. To be honest with you, I still can't see a nun in her garb without feeling a surge of resentment. But since most nuns today go about in mufti I don't have that unpleasant sensation as often as I once did.

RD. Were they really so mean that you were permanently scarred?

SC. Yes, they were mean, to boys at least. Girls could get away with a lot; boys were on a very short leash.

RD. Did they employ corporal punishment as you relate?

SC. Not Corporal; they applied Major punishment! Believed it was good for our souls. I know many catholic school graduates, men and women. The women went through a period of experimentation and searching but returned to the fold with zeal once they turned matronly. Almost all the men are lost.

Sam Culotta

RD. Are you lost, as you call it?

SC. Oddly enough, no, but I doubt Sister Mary Leonice would agree with my new, improved Catholicism.

RD. Interesting. Later stories, most notably, "Transcontinental Divide" and "Why Is He Being Quiet" clearly reflect a certain amount of discomfort with authority figures. Does this stem from your Catholic school experience?

SC. From that, and from my Sicilian upbringing, a tendency toward anarchy. It's been a continuing problem for me. The fact that I survived, even had success, in the military, should mean something. I guess I can do it when I have to.

RD. Yet, you went on to have a successful marriage and a successful career in banking.

SC. Yes, in spite of myself.

RD. Ha! To what do you attribute this?

SC. I lean toward anarchy but have an almost compulsive need to avoid trouble because I fear that if I ever let go it could result in my being put into the hands of the very people I resent.

RD. I see. You're a very complex person, Sam.

SC. We're all complex people, Rad, all different but the same.

Clueless In Paradise

RD. I suppose so. Now, I'm curious about "The Chicken Came First". This is what you would characterize as an essay, correct?

SC. Correct.

RD. OK. Do you have a background in philosophy? Other stories indicate you were a pre-med student at one time but there is no mention of philosophy.

SC. That's a great question Rad. The answer is no. I've read some books on the subject like Will Durant's Story of Philosophy, and I had a lower division course in which the students spent more time staring at each other until our auras appeared than discussing the thoughts of the philosophers. I love philosophy and I have an unquenchable thirst to learn about it; unfortunately, I lack the intellect it requires. I always get philosophers confused with one another and when I do study the subject, it doesn't stick in my brain.

RD. I see. But that didn't stop you from venturing forth into that arcane field of study in your essay. You answer the age-old question of the Chicken/Egg with some irony, but little reticence. Your conclusion is convincing, I must say, but let's not give it away here.

SC. Really, you found it convincing? I can't tell you how pleased I am to hear that. Funny thing is, the notion first came to me decades ago. It finally came together in this essay. You will note that I close with an impressive cop out, if I say so myself. I wouldn't want anyone to think I really know what the hell I'm talking about.

RD. Heh, heh. I suppose "Oh Lucky Us" was another bit of philosophical riffing? The element of random chance is certainly your subject here, yes?

SC. Chance drives me nuts. I wrote a terrible short story years ago about a guy who is a creature of habit. He's a rock hound and goes to a rock hound convention. While in town he follows his compulsive routines, one of which includes always walking out in the morning to the store in whatever town he is in, to buy the local town newspaper. On his way back to his motel he gets in the way of a bullet from a country boy who has just had a terrible fight with his wife. And it goes on from there. I share Woody Allen's view that the world is filled with potential disaster. But at least he's funny about it.

RD. You make that abundantly clear in this one and you do it with just enough humor to avoid the impression that you're a raving neurotic.

SC. Thank you, I guess. I don't mind being a neurotic, but I'd rather not be seen as a raving neurotic.

RD. Leaving the philosophical and psychological now, I'd like to discuss the overall scheme of "Sleeping With Lumbago" before getting to the really fun stuff about your family and your time in the Air Force. There is a convenient chronology to the stories.

Clueless In Paradise

They began in your grade school years continue through your years of transition, (you and your family move across the country from Rochester, New York to the Los Angeles area when you're thirteen), adjustment, often painful, and on through adulthood including your military service, marriage, banking career and, finally, retirement. Have I left anything out?

SC. Well, yes, but you hit the high points. That's fine.

RD. My question is: At the outset, did you intend to create a memoir and to present it in chronological order?

SC I'd already written a family memoir and I wanted this to document my personal ideas and notions of living life. If I had literary aspirations and unmitigated gall, I'd say "Lumbago" is on the order of Montaigne's essays. Sarah Bakewell recently wrote a fine book on his life and titled it "How To Live." Mine would be more like: "How *I* Live."

RD. I see. So, there's a certain amount of free-wheeling here which, I might suggest, gives your stories their folksy, home-grown quality.

SC. Ha! I've never heard it put that way, but yes, I'll go along with what you say. On the other hand, if we were discussing this in an undergrad survey course, we might refer to it as the product of a mind unfettered by the formalities learned in writers' courses and seminars, a bit like Grandma Moses' primitivism. Can I be honest here, Rad?

RD. Of course you can, Sam.

Sam Culotta

SC. Then, let me say that writing these stories was so easy they can't possibly be very good. A writer should sit with furrowed brow with half empty whiskey bottles and an ashtray full of cigarette butts. He or she should bemoan their periodic dry spells, writer's block; they should be able to recount battles with their publishers and editors. Writing this book was like falling off a log. Sorry if this offends any real writers listening out there, but it's the truth. Of course, there is a trade-off. Think about it: would you rather struggle to write creatively when you're in your twenties and thirties when your intellectual development is not yet fully formed and your experience is shallow, or would you rather wait until you're in your sixties and seventies so you can write with a fully formed outlook and the freedom of not giving a damn. And even better, not in financial need.

RD. (Laughing). I'm sorry, Sam; I'm laughing because of the freshness and honesty of your attitude. I appreciate your self assessment but, as you must know, the final assessment will be that of your readers, and the reviews I've read indicate that they have taken your stories to heart and have seen themselves reflected in them. This indicates you have tapped into an area that is shared by almost everyone. I was particularly drawn to stories such as, "Why Is He Being So Quiet?", and "Transcontinental Divide" which explore the element of alienation, a phenomena we all share and can relate to easily. And, of course, there are the wonderful memoir-like stories of your early years in Rochester and later, in Southern California with your wonderful family, particularly your larger than life father. There is the special quality of being raised in a blue-

Clueless In Paradise

collar, second generation Sicilian family, and yet, just as with individuals, uniqueness is easily relatable to those of us who come from quite different backgrounds. Tell us a bit more about your father.

SC. More? I don't know what more there is. He was a simple man, a blue-collar automotive genius who could diagnose a bad carburetor or valve in a passing car. He was brusque, coarse, highly opinionated, loving, insensitive at times, too sensitive at other times; he was relatively uneducated but thought he had the answer to everything and was more than willing to share it with you whether you were interested or not. He was often irritated or angry with my mother but would not let her go to sleep without telling her he loved her and hearing her say she loved him. Like I said, he was a simple man.

RD. Well, that doesn't sound simple to me.

SC. That's my point; no one is really simple. On the first day of my Microbiology class, the professor held up a small container of cow manure and said: "There is more romance going on in this little container of manure than in the entire student body." Imagine that: all that going on in a blob of cow manure. So, imagine how complex the lives of humans are. I never forgot that.

RD. That's very interesting; I never thought of it that way.

SC. Great poetry does it best but I don't have that particular talent so I have to do it the only way I can.

Sam Culotta

RD. Have you written any poetry?

SC. I've turned out a few poems that are more than crap but less than polished. I was unfortunate enough to be published in a regional magazine the first time I submitted my poems.

RD. Unfortunate? That's remarkable; most people have to submit many poems to many magazines before they get published, and many people never get published.

SC. Unfortunate because it made me think I was a poet. Next thing you know, you're turning out wretched stuff thinking it's good. The first thing a poet should learn is that not every poem he or she writes is poetic. Even the best and most successful writers of poetry, prose or music end up getting some things published that would never be accepted from an unknown writer. You know what they are. I'm sure you've read or heard them. I should add though that I've been working with poetry more lately. I attribute it to my recent relationship with a few poets through a Facebook group. (Strange as it sounds.) One in particular the poet, Joe Green, whom I mention in the dedication of "Lumbago" has shown me by example that there is a style of poetry that suits my temperament, a style based on the same emotions that drive me to memoir, a style which incorporates humor in the most natural and felicitous way. So, look out!

RD. Fair warning, Sam! I wish you great success.

RD. Now, back to your stories for a moment. Are there some writers who have been major influences?

Clueless In Paradise

SC. Wow, that's a tough one. There are many. Remember, I've been reading for a very long time. I get something from almost everyone I read, but there are a few examples that stand out. Nabokov and Orwell were amazing. Both wrote lucid, brilliant prose and in Nabokov's case, did it in a language other than his mother tongue. Some of their sentences should be under glass in a museum of literature.

Then there is Philip Roth. I drool at his ability to compose page, page and a half paragraphs without loss of control; he manages to maintain coherence while constructing a rich, complex jungle of words, yet never gets lost. At the other end of the spectrum is Kurt Vonnegut, Jr. whose sentences and paragraphs are spare, and exquisite. And I haven't even mentioned James Joyce... don't even get me started on him.

At a more practical level, I was drawn to the work of David Sedaris because not only is he funny, he's wry and slightly bruised. I won't say I used him as a model so much as that I found in him a kindred spirit. My writing style, (if I may be bold enough to proclaim a "style"), developed a similar tone even before I read his books.

RD. Yes, you describe the book as, and I quote: " the unexceptional life of an unexceptional man with an exceptional amount of wit and discontent."
I guess the discontent is what you're getting at.

SC. Yes, it is.

RD. That's very interesting. Did you have some say in the description the publisher used?

SC. Well, I wrote it, so I guess the answer is, yes.

RD. You wrote it?

SC. Yes. That's how it works with print on demand publication, you provide almost everything and they make adjustments or corrections as needed. That's only if they're a quality on-demand publisher. In this case, they provided editing (for a price) and helped design the cover. Since my book was chosen as an "Editor's Choice" candidate, it required professional editing. When I published Family Suite, I had to produce everything and there was no professional edit.

RD. I'm sorry, I should have mentioned that Lumbago was awarded "Editor's Choice", I'm sure that pleased you; it distinguishes your product from others, I presume.

SC. It's easy to overlook. They put a little emblem on the bottom of the back cover. Considering what it took to earn it, the reward is minimal. As far as distinction is concerned, I was informed that only about ten percent of submissions are made eligible for Editor's Choice. You can take that with a grain of salt.

RD. Ha, ha. "Family Suite" is the memoir and family history you wrote earlier. Is that book available for sale?

SC. No, it isn't. In that case I intended to produce a document that my friends and relatives could have for their pleasure and, if appropriate, for reference should any of them or their descendants decide to write a further family history. I printed only the number I needed.

Clueless In Paradise

RD. I see. Well, based on what I read of "Sleeping With Lumbago" I'm sure Family Suite is an entertaining and informative book as well. Have you considered making it available commercially?

SC. Oh, no. There are some chapters that might appeal to a broader readership, but for the most part it's about our families and would not interest most people. In fact, based on the deafening silence from some of my distant relatives, I'm not sure it interested even them.

RD. Ha! Well, what's next for you? Do you have another project in the works?

SC. I'm always doodling around with short pieces, essays and even poems. I have some work in the bag, as I mentioned, some of the poems show signs of life. You never know, maybe a book with both poems and essays. But, seriously, I doubt if I will do another one. Of course, if your listeners respond to this show by running out to buy my book I'm sure it will inspire me to give it serious consideration.

RD. I hope that is the case, Sam. Our listeners are an eclectic bunch; from the correspondence I receive, I'd say they have a broad range of literary interests and are always on watch for something fresh and stimulating and I can assure them "Sleeping With Lumbago" is just that.

SC. Thank you, Rad.

RD. I'm certain you will continue to view the world through the same lens you have in the past and hope that the urge to record your opinions and experiences may prove to be overwhelming. Somehow, I suspect we can expect to see more from you.

SC. From your mouth to God's ear, as they say. I appreciate your appreciation.

RD. You're very welcome.

I wish we had more time to talk; I wanted to get to your Air Force experiences and your banking career, both of which you confronted in the same nonconventional manner you've dealt with everything else in your life. Let me just assure readers that these stories are just as distinctive as the earlier ones about his younger years. And don't forget to look for the joke in the last story, "The Spinal Chronicles".

Once again, our guest today was Sam R. Culotta. The book is, "Sleeping With Lumbago", Often humorous, always personal stories, (or, essays if you prefer). It is available in hardcover, paperback and e-book formats and can be found at Amazon.com, Barnes and Noble.com. popular e-book retailers and, of course, at the publisher's website.

Thank you again for appearing on our broadcast. I wish you success with your book and I look forward to seeing more from you in the future.

SC. I thank you and KRNK radio for having me. I think I had fun.

RD. Ha, ha, ha,..I know I did!

Please stay tuned. We'll be right back after a short intermission for a conversation with our next guest ....

The End of the Beginning

> We shall not cease from exploration
> And the end of all our exploring
> Will be to arrive where we started
> And know the place for the first time.
> T.S. Eliot

I'm not sure what PoMo actually entails other than the author's being intrusive. It's fun for a while, but then I get tired of wondering what's fiction and what's real. When I read Fowles' "The French Lieutenant's Woman" I didn't even realize I was reading something like that. When he provided different endings for what was a captivating plot, I thought it was interesting in an *avant garde* sort of way. Imagine my surprise when I learned later it was post modernism. In fact, it's considered to be a specific type of postmodernism known as "historiographic metafiction" which, according to Wikipedia (a source I rely on in this case because I'm lazy), refers to "well-known and popular novels which are both intensely self-reflexive and yet paradoxically also lay claim to historical events and personages" How's that for a mouthful of lit-speak?

    Maybe it's my advanced age that encourages me to express disdain for established literary norms. Perhaps it's only my way of laying the foundation for the excuse I'm going to need when this is complete. Have you ever done something like that when you're about to undertake a daunting task? I sometimes notify my tennis opponent that I had a lousy night's sleep because the grandchildren slept over. If the match goes

Clueless In Paradise

south I can shake my head as though I'm getting out the cobwebs. I don't' know you but I'd bet you've done something similar sometime in your life. Let us see where the road leads. Ask not, it leads to thee...apologies to John Donne.

Donne was one of the first poets to capture my imagination. I've always been drawn to the ones who use language in previously unconventional ways Gerard Manley Hopkins comes to mind. I've tried to write like every poet or novelist I've ever read but it keeps coming out like me, the way *I* write. I'm learning to live with this unhappy realization. I want to make clear right now that I don't call myself a writer. I write, but that's not the same thing, but you probably know that already.

Have you heard the one about Iraq? We went there over a decade ago to free them from the tyrannical rule of Saddam Hussein. (The Bushes pronounced Saddam, Sad-damn.) They were pretty funny, the Bushes. Well, the old man was; the son was funny but not in a good way. Anyway, we dropped 1.7 trillion dollars and lost the lives of close to five thousand American troops. Tens of thousands more have come home wounded in body and mind. We destroyed the Iraqi government and infrastructure, and liberated their people. Unfortunately, tens of thousands of Iraqis were "liberated" from their mortal coils .A while ago we departed from there. We felt confident they could govern themselves and protect their citizens from terrorism. The country is now being torn apart by sectarian warfare. One Islamic sect doesn't like the other Islamic sect so the one is trying to take over the country from the other which happens to be governing the country. Iraq, like much of that part of the world is composed of tribal groups.

If this is news to you, that's understandable but it appears it was also mews to the brain trust who led us into that cesspool of misery and violence. That, or they were just crazy, take your pick. It's not like they should not have known; after World War I, the British stitched Iraq together like Frankenstein's monster giving no consideration to the fact that they were suturing hostile tribal groups together. The idea was to make them a cohesive nation that would provide Britain with a safe, cheap source of petroleum. The Bush administration must have suffered from the same delusion; they felt certain the access to cheap oil would more than pay for the expenses of the war. That may have constituted a political screed on my part for which I apologize profusely.

One of my favorite books of poetry is "Delusions, etc." by John Berryman. The first section is built on a series of poems that correspond with the "Hours" of the church, you know: Lauds, Matins, Prime, Interstitial Office, Tierce, Sext, Nones, Vespers and Compline. The book is rife with religious exclamations, ironic given that Berryman threw off belief years before. Here's something I really love:

> "*Lord, have mercy on my son: for he is lunatik,*
> *and sore vexed: for oftimes he falleth into*
>   *the fire and oft into the water.*
> *And he did evil, because he prepared not*
>   *his heart to seek the Lord.*

Clueless In Paradise

Berryman put this before the text of the book and did not accredit it. I'm told it's from "Matthew" or "Chronicles", or something like that.

The first real book I ever read was Booth Tarkington's "Penrod and Sam". My aunt gave it to me when I was very young because I seemed precocious. I remember reading it, so I guess I was. Books have always held a special place in my heart. As a boy, I walked what seemed miles to the Lincoln Library in my home town of Rochester, N.Y. I had no guidance so I just picked up whatever interested me: books about musical instruments, story books, adventures, sports, etc.. In winter, I often returned home in the dusk with my treasure trove of reading material. No bespectacled nerd, I; I was very active in sports and devilry, but found time to read and play my accordion.

Yes, my accordion. But that's another story. Suffice it to say, it didn't take, much to my father's disappointment. He felt better about me when I became a banker and got a college degree. He would ask me once a year what I was making. At some point in my career, I gave him the figure and he gave a sigh of satisfaction. "Good, now I won't worry about you anymore." I don't know why that number satisfied him, but knowing how he thought there was undoubtedly some arbitrary income that he considered adequate and I had reached it. I was married, had two children and was an officer of the bank by then; I'm glad I was able to satisfy him eventually.

".. vile rock of melancholy, a disease so frequent, as few there are that feel not the smart of it."

Sam Culotta

That's from Sir Richard Burton, 19th Century explorer, adventurer and man of letters. I've suffered from that ailment all my life to some degree, but a few years ago I thought I should mention it to my doctor. I think I'm sorry I did, but to admit that would be to feel unhappy that I exposed myself to the cursed cure: antidepressants. I don't think I'm happier, just less volatile, also less creative, less ambitious and less interesting, even to myself. Less ambitious may be overstating the matter; I've never been possessed of great ambition. In this I am my father's son. Like him, I'll work my tail off and perform well, but only because I want to be done with whatever the job is. I doubt I ever have, or ever will, realize my "potential". I hate the word and its irritating cousin "attitude", probably because I've been hearing all my life about my failure to reach the former and my disregard for the latter. Now I'm of a certain age where I can look back and see that I accomplished more than enough to qualify as successful. My god, if I had reached my potential *and* harnessed my bad attitude there is no telling to what heights I may have risen. When all is said and done, you get what you need, it's just that some people need more than others.

It's mid afternoon and I'm feeling low. The hours between one and four have always let me down. They are the Tuesday's of the day, the middle of a long book; they lack the fresh optimism of morning and the comforting capitulation of evening. On the job, lunch is over, the system wants to wind down, but there are hours to go before you can quit. They are the dog days of summer, bereft of spring's promise and

Clueless In Paradise

autumn's glorious flame-out. I think they are the hours when most people die but I have yet to find supporting evidence. Maybe what I feel is simply a premonition of my own passing. I know that whatever ails me is always worse during these hours: fever, depression, boredom, pain, lethargy. I point out that Jesus was hung on the cross and died between twelve noon and three p.m. Just saying. (How does that translate to Pacific Standard Time, I wonder?) I'm not sure how the religious determined the times, but I'll accept them as support for my claim.

Dorothy Parker said that beauty may be only skin deep but ugly goes clean to the bone. For a few days I've been seeing a "vintage" Chrysler sitting on an auto transporter. These are the days of retro worship; take an old beater, resurrect it and it becomes a "classic" worth many times its original value. This one could be anything from a '57 to a '60. I'm not sufficiently interested to examine it that closely because I try to keep my distance from grotesqueries. The three year range is indicative of the design problem. When the 1957 models came out, Chrysler Corporation touted their line of Plymouth, Dodge and Chrysler as "1960 new". It had, and still has, an *outré* look: futuristic sweep-back styling that manages to look low and wide, It was as long as a short aircraft carrier but not nearly as graceful. The adventurous styling remained virtually unchanged through 1960, thus making good on the company's promise.

An Air Force friend of mine had the '60 model and I remember sitting in it and marveling at the oblong steering wheel, the lunatic-safe padded dash and the tundra-like expanse of interior. New or even newish cars have always caused the blood of young men to rush, the heart to beat faster. All I recall from my experience was sympathy for the poor schmuck. This was the most ungainly automobile I had ever encountered. The one I pass on the street these days has acquired no cachet at all from its vintage status. It represents the worst of American taste: complete lack of charm, utility sacrificed for design, (if design is an appropriate term in this case), and as clueless to resource abuse as humanly possible. Yes, the ugly goes clean to the bone

Most of what I write, essays or poems, turn out to be memoir-ish even if unintended. But memoir is a form of nostalgia and nostalgia can be a trap. At this point in my life the euphoria of spring is a fading memory, more wistful thinking than anything. Even autumn, my favorite season, while still fresh in my mind lives in the rearview mirror. This doesn't make me miserable or bitter; I have gained enough perspective to appreciate the onset of winter. What's not to like about a chilly wind outside and a warm fire within. I'm not certain if we learn to love the slowing down and comfort of our age or if we accept it because to do otherwise would be to wander madly on the heath, cursing our fate. Every day is just a day, whether it's a day in our fifth or our seventy-fifth year. When someone told Los Angeles Dodgers' Hall of Fame manager, Tommy Lasorda, they had had a long day, Tommy would remind them that there is no such thing; every day has only twenty four hours. So, I have to be on guard. There's nothing wrong with looking back with affection and warmth, just don't get trapped there while you're visiting. Another reference: Woody Allen's "Midnight In Paris". When the character finds a way to slip back into the age of Hemingway, Gertrude Stein,

Clueless In Paradise

F. Scott Fitzgerald and their generation he meets and falls in love with a woman from that time. Soon, he learns that she is nostalgic for the Gay Nineties. Check the rear-view mirror, but remember you're still hurtling down the road.

I live in a suburbs of Los Angeles and like all California suburbs the population is ever shifting and becoming more diverse by the year. Although I've lived here for many years, there are only a few people I know: the neighbors on my cul de sac and a few more from the surrounding area. That's about it. When I go out into the community I seldom meet people I know, even in the local stores. I recognize some, I see them in restaurants and the library, or standing in line at the movies, but we never exchange a word or gesture of recognition. My daily walks with the dog have brought me into contact with a few people who live on the streets nearby and we often exchange casual greetings. But there are others who will not lift their heads to make eye contact. I can understand that women out walking or jogging on their own may be reluctant to share a look and a smile, after all, predators do exist and women are the usual prey. Teenagers are often told by their parents to be wary of strangers, and others are just unwilling to speak to anyone older than themselves. There are, however, guys like me walking along or riding bikes, and they act as though I'm not even there. Some may have poor language skills or come from cultures where looking at strangers is considered rude, but I think most are just socially maladroit and they piss me off.

That's a problem of mine: I get pissed off too often and too easily. I notice when I'm on the treadmill at the gym and I monitor my heart rate that it goes up ten or so points whenever I see Fox News on one of the TV's they have going. I try to set up in front of ESPN, or at worst, CNN, but when the machines are busy there's not much choice.

Endings are difficult, all sorts of endings. The best ending to a novel, in my humble opinion, is in James Joyce's *Finnegans Wake* where the closing sentence runs right back to the opening sentence: "*riverrun past eve and adams*".

When something that great has been done by someone that great, only a fool would dare to go there. I have so much more to think about.

List Of Books, Stories And Phrases Important To My Life

I read a great article by the late William Gass in which he described twelve books he found to be the most important books in his life. Like all such lists there is a great deal of subjectivity involved. (Ask a hundred people to give you a top ten favorite books list and stand back.) After I read the article I began to think about some books, stories, and other works that impressed me to the extent that I have never forgotten them. If my choices pale beside those of Gass, I can assure you I was no less impacted by mine than he was by his.

Penrod and Sam, by Booth Tarkington.

What I remember most about this book is its very existence. In my house there were no books of note, if there were any at all. The only books I read were comic books and school books. (The Baltimore Catechism may be imaginative in its own right but is not entertaining at all.) My Aunt Adeline was a reader of popular novels and noticed my precocious reading ability. At my next birthday she gave me Penrod and Sam. It was a seminal moment in my young life and therefore, worthy of mention.

Archie Comics

Sam Culotta

A popular comic book in the Forties and Fifties. In its pages I recognized the discomfort I had been experiencing at school as unrequited love.

Encyclopedia of Medicine (1950's edition)

I found a dusty copy of a Hygiene book in our attic. It peaked my interest in matters of "hygiene" but answered few of my questions. My Aunt's encyclopedia was a treasure trove of sexual information. I learned there were seven acceptable positions for intercourse. I gathered definitive information on the act itself. This is *very* important knowledge for a pre-teen boy in the early 1950's.

ULYSSES by James Joyce

Ulysses was the first book I read which could be considered "literature". When I was sixteen, I ran across it in a nearby public library. I opened it to the short history of the novel, its being banned, its being snuck into the U.S. and finally, the famous pornography trial and the James M. Woolsey decision declaring it to be a legitimate work of art and not pornographic. Moments later I was sprinting home to read it.

I will admit that at age 16 and devoid of higher learning, I had no idea just what the hell I was reading, but the parts I did grasp changed me forever. I've read it in its entirety three times since, gaining more understanding and appreciation each time. I now have an entire shelf of Joyce: all his works, the Richard Ellman biography and various other Joyce related books. Ulysses remains my "desert island" choice.

Silas Marner, The Weaver of Raveloe by George Eliot

I doubt I would have read this book ever had it not been assigned by my high school Senior English teacher. The story of a 19th century man living in a slum area of Northern England, Marner is a Calvinist who lives alone caring for an aging deacon. No thanks! This was my first exposure to this type of literature and as I read it I found myself fully engrossed. Marner accused of a crime he didn't commit, is forced to leave his humble lodgings and resettle in a rural area where his is unknown. He takes up his weavers trade and in an isolation I found strangely appealing, begins to hoard the gold pieces he earns. As the novel goes on events bring great change and eventual contentment.

    It is the lonely existence and the slow, dogged financial progress that captivated me. To this day I cannot explain why I identified with our humble hero. I was seventeen at the time and like most teenagers felt a sense of isolation, so maybe that was the hook. This much I know, it's been over sixty years since I read it and when I considered this list of books it was right there.

A Generation of Vipers by Philip Wylie

"In this 1942 volume, Wylie, one of the founders of *The New Yorker*, attacks everything imaginable, from politics to religion to mothers. He could give H.L Mencken a run for his money as the most opinionated person of the 20th century. Considering the world hasn't improved much in the last 50 years, much of what he says has great relevance today." -- *Library Journal*

I couldn't say it better. I Ran across a paperback edition of this in the mid to late 50's. To my, questioning teenaged mind it was a bolt of lightning. At one point he's discussing the moral hypocrisy of modern advertising as it assumed a greater and greater part of American culture's splurge of materialism. He offers the observation that all those ads and billboards aimed at inducing the "new woman" to buy glamour products pose one, and only one, question to their targets: "are you a good lay?". At another point he goes after the Catholic Church's practice of saving the baby at the cost of the mother's life, going so far as to describe a scene where a priest anoints the yet to be born baby vaginally. All these years later Wylie's book still has the power to enflame cultural and religious opinions. It certainly appealed to the latent revolutionary in me.

The Cry and the Covenant, by Mortan Thompson. Pub. 1949. A novelized biography of Austrian doctor, Ignaz Semmelweis (b. 1818 - d. 1865).

I read this gripping novel during the time I still believed I would become a pre-med major. Subsequent exposure to advanced mathematics disabused me of the notion. But I was, and remain, impressed by the doctor's struggle to overcome ignorance in the face of factual evidence. Sound familiar? In 1847, while working in a medical clinic where women were sent to give birth, " he found if doctors just washed their hands in chlorine solution, the death rate for Puerperal fever (which is caused by sepsis) could be brought down to less the 1%." At that time the death rate was running at 35%. The book planted the idea that good does not win out without a struggle which often includes punishing the source.

The Conversion of the Jews.. a short story from Goodbye Columbus and Five Short Stories, by Philip Roth.

Roth's first published book was a critical and popular success. To use the cliché: he burst onto the literary scene. I read the book years after he was an established, critically acclaimed author, long after Sabbath's Theater, long after the Zuckerman novels and the American Trilogy. I read it when Library of America published the Roth collected works. Thought I may as well go back to the beginning. Remarkable to me and, I suppose, to book critics was how mature the young writer was from the very start. His writing was that of someone with a greater store of life experience. His style and his world view seemed to arrive full blown, as did the talents of other great writers and artists.

While none of his short stories measures up to Joyce's "The Dead" from "The Dubliners", like it, "The Conversion of the Jews" contains themes that appear in virtually every other book he wrote. Told from the point of view of Oscar Freedman, thirteen, there is the confrontational questioner of religious belief, the sensualist, the intellectual questioner of all things and the willingness to accept isolation even while needing validation. Jewish middle-class Oscar should have met Salinger's Holden Caulfield. Of course, they would have run in entirely different socioeconomic circles and perhaps despised one another.

Bekenntrusse des Hochstaplers Felix Krull. Der Memoiren, erster Teil.
An unfinished novel by Thomas Mann. Later translated from German as: **Confessions of Felix Krull, Confidence Man**

Sam Culotta

So, why is this lesser known and unfinished novel by the great Thomas Mann on this list? Because it was one of two German novels I read as assignments in my fourth semester German class. Our numbers that semester had started at an already diminished 12 students and quickly dwindled to 6 or 7, so our beloved professor, Herr Ninneman decided we should meet in his study. There, with fresh coffee and donuts or cookies, we spoke only German, listened to German Opera on the phonograph machine and read German books. I had never before and have never since, enjoyed such an informal scholastic environment. The experience was marvelous.

We first read *Drei Männer Im Schnee,* by Erich Kästner, a light, comic work intended for German school children and enjoyed by adults. But it was Felix Krull, more challenging and more "adult" that I remember enjoying most. The details of the story are not important to me now. The fact that I can say I read it and a book by the great Thomas Mann, *in German* is rewarding enough.

The Iceman Cometh, a play by Eugene O'Neill

I had a professor of English tell the class that she loved prose and drama but poetry was to her more of an occasional crush. My own tastes would place drama in that final category but that is not to take a thing away from drama like The Iceman Cometh.

The scenes take place in a saloon where a group of alcoholics gather regularly to discuss their problems, chief among them, their addictions and how they are coping or not coping. Most have dreams of recovery and return to a successful life, but they realize they will probably never achieve them. The highlight of their lives is the annual or semi-annual visits of Theodore Hickman, known to them as "Hickey", a successful salesman and man about town, he is looked up to by the destitute bunch. Expectations are high he will show up this night because it's the saloonkeeper Harry's birthday.

When Hickey does arrive he seems different, he is troubled. He begins haranguing them for wasting their lives. He tells them to stop their useless dreaming. He says he has given up drinking and leading an immoral life. He has reason to feel guilty. After years of philandering and otherwise abusing his good wife, Evelyn, the woman he fell in love with when they were both young, he could no longer stand the fact that she continued to forgive his bad behavior. He discloses that Evelyn has died. After making up reasons for her death, he breaks down and admits he killed her earlier that very evening. His explanation is astounding:

He killed her because *she deserved better than him*. He killed her to free her from the pain his constant betrayals and drunkenness caused her. He killed her because *she loved him too much*!

"And then I saw I'd always known that was the only possible way to give her peace and free her from the misery of loving me. I saw it meant peace for me too, knowing she was at peace. I felt as though a ton of guilt was lifted off my mind. I remember I stood by the bed and suddenly I had to laugh. I couldn't help it, and I knew Evelyn would forgive me. I remember I heard myself speaking to her, as if it was something I'd always wanted to say. Well, you know what you can do with your pipe dream now, you damned bitch!' "

We could discuss the hatful of Freudian goodies for hours, but I prefer to let this amazing bit of inwit speak for itself.

Sam Culotta

"Two Concepts of Liberty" an essay from "The Proper Study of Man" by Isaiah Berlin

Philosophy has always fascinated me, but like Aesop's grapes, it dangles just out of my intellectual reach. When I discovered this book by Isaiah Berlin I found at least two of the essays therein more approachable than most philosophical writing. That is not to say I've grasped the grapes, but I've gotten close enough to touch them with my fingertips.

In **"Two Concepts of Liberty"** Berlin addresses the definition of "freedom" (which he uses interchangeably with "liberty"): What is it, how is it achieved, perceived, put to use? To condense the issue he divides freedom into "negative liberty" and "positive liberty". It can get confusing because it turns out that, in this case, "negative" is the more positive form of freedom and "positive"... well, you get the point.

Negative liberty concerns freedom *from* coercion or any other means to interfere with individual freedoms. My first reaction was: "Hey, what the heck? I thought Berlin was a liberal philosopher! This sounds like a conservative, even libertarian point of view." Well, it's not. Because he goes on to point out that in any sort of political or social system, some freedoms must be sacrificed in what could be described as a trade-off. (Echoes of Hobbes?) Positive liberty, on the other hand, may begin as a wish to take the initiative in bringing about a better society, but too often becomes overbearing until it arrives at a place where these self- realization folks decide that other people are not cutting it, resulting in coercion and forms of authoritarianism.

Clueless In Paradise

Berlin experienced authoritarian rule first hand: born in Riga, Latvia, in 1909, to a Jewish family, he moved to Petrograd, Russia at age seven where he witnessed the "October Revolt" also known as "Red October" in 1917 which brought the Bolsheviks to power. Later, he witnessed the rise of Nazi Fascism and Adolf Hitler. It is not surprising that he had strong views about liberty and freedom.

"Liberty for the wolves is death to the lambs". ...

CLUELESS IN PARADISE

EIGHT DAYS OF FUN IN SICILY

Preflight

I've never made up a bucket list. It may be my native indolence or the fact that at my age there aren't a lot of things I want to do, or places I want to go or sights I want to see. If I did make up one, it would likely have one item only: Visit Italy, specifically Sicily. So when my sister told me she planned to go there and that she wanted me to go with her, my bluff was called.

My wife would love to see Europe but has a numbing terror of flight over large bodies of water. She isn't a fan of flying anyway, but over the water is particularly fearsome to her. I have tried and tried to help her realize that when a plane goes down it doesn't really matter what it hits, but to no avail. She doesn't want fishies picking at her toes under any circumstances. Because of this, my going would mean leaving my beloved for a longer time than we have ever been apart during our many years together. At the same time, I was reluctant to disappoint my sister who had been widowed some months earlier and was deserving of a trip of a lifetime, a chance to unwind.

Clueless In Paradise

Our families hail from that beautiful and ancient Mediterranean isle, Sicily. Our father's family are from Cefalù, our mother's from the Agrigento area. By now any remaining family members may be too old or too young to have much interest in a couple of shirt-tail relatives from America, but the idea that we might run into a few of them is irresistible. Some years ago I spoke with a gentleman who shared my name. That Sam Culotta hailed from Cefalù and visited there every few years. He assured me I would love the city and would meet long lost relatives. We compared family histories: he told me his grandfather had owned and operated the general store/blacksmith shop. My great grandfather raised mules for the Italian army for a period of time, so it didn't take much imagination to conclude that he may very well have had his mules shoed by this man's grandfather! Our conversation piqued my desire to go there at the time.

We don't leave for six weeks so we have plenty of time to confuse ourselves with guide books. I am trying to gather as much Italian as I can cram into that short period of time but hope there are plenty of English speakers among the population to keep us out of trouble. We will spend eight days travelling to cities and villages from Palermo southwest to the coast at Realmonte and then a bit inland to Agrigento, the homeland of our maternal grandparents, the LaFrancas, down and around to Siricusa, up the eastern coast to Taormina, then back across the north coast to Cefalù before returning to Palermo the night before our return flight home. If time and conditions permit we may even visit Mt. Etna, the emblematic landmark of the famed Sicilian temperament.

I've purchased a discreet money belt that features slim design and the ability to resist the rays of electronic credit card readers. The guide books tell us that Palermo, for one, is home to some of the world's most skilled pick pockets and thieves. The books also recommend travelers not ask about the mafia, which still thrives throughout much of Sicily. (As recently as 2012 the merchants of one moderate-sized city were forced to make strategic departures for a while after relationships with the local mafia leaders became strained.) But these precautions and concerns aside, we are eager to visit our family's homeland.

The Adventure Begins

> It's a long way from L.A. to Roma
> It's a long time to hang in the sky.
> (apologies to the late, great John Denver)

Wednesday, 9/27/17

Our Al Italia non-stop flight to Rome, Italy, was scheduled to take off at 4:15 PM. We arranged for an airport shuttle service to pick us up at Patti's house, so Terri drove me over there and waited with us until we left. As we pulled away I was reminded of leaving her at the airport all those years ago when I left for the Air Force on Christmas Eve, 1961. Fifty-four years have passed and the feeling hadn't changed. I learned later that she felt the same way and even choked up a bit as our shuttle turned the corner and left. Ah, the flame still burns.

Clueless In Paradise

    Once we hit the road my mind turned toward the trip ahead: I expected a mixture of excitement, exhilaration, tension, frustration, and general discomfort, and I was correct. Checking in was relatively uneventful. My large luggage bag had a flattened wheel, a souvenir of my last trip: a cruise to Alaska.
Sounds like a small inconvenience but it turned out to be a source of irritation and/or humor every time I had to pull it across an airport or a hotel lobby. The damned thing sounded like a cross between a jack hammer and a semi-automatic rifle, not the most felicitous sound to the ears of travelers and TSA agents. I dragged it along cursing under my breath while my sister choked back laughter.
    The aircraft was a Boeing 777, the one with triple seats along both sides and rows of six seats along the center. It is a huge thing designed to accommodate the maximum number of passengers with the least amount of passenger space. Fortunately for us, we were in the aisle and center seats. Fortunate because each window seat has a metal box of electronic controls for the seat counsels where your feet should be. The box was just large enough to cause the passenger to sit slightly twisted. But they did have the window which could be seen through on occasion.
    Despite what every cell in my brain told me was impossible, the behemoth left mother earth graceful as a seagull and rode the air gently. Of course, eleven hours can be an eternity when you can't extend your legs without endangering the steady stream of passengers to and from the battery of toilets in back. And these same people could be counted upon to sway with just the needed alacrity to knock your elbow off the arm of the seat. The food service was more dependable than the quality of the food. I expected more

from an Italian airlines, but all in all, the flight was as good as could be expected.

Patti was befriended by her seatmate, a young woman returning from Los Angeles to her home in Slovakia. She enjoyed L.A. very much, had made friends and was sorry to leave there. Turns out she travels all over the world and although she was sorry to be heading home, I hoped she would be happy to see her family again. By the time we landed in Rome Patti had forged a relationship with her, even taking her name and exchanging emails. My sister is by far the most sociable of the two of us.

Thursday, 9/28/17

Roma

Due to the time change, it was Wednesday in our bodies but Thursday, 9/28, on the clock. I wish I could say we saw Rome, or were actually *in* Rome, but all we saw were some grassy areas with trees as we came in for a landing. We were safely down in plenty of time for us to relax a bit before we boarded the short flight to Palermo, Sicily. The lurch in time zones took its toll on us; it was now a day later even though we were still living a day sooner.

All this was exhausting and we were worse for wear. We ventured off to find our gate. On the way, we exchanged some dollars for Euros via an ATM machine. I managed to carry out my first ever international purchase but in the process left at least two euros on the cashier's counter. How was I supposed to know that there are such things as one and two euro coins! She got a great tip for a two euro bottle of orange juice.

Once we were settled in the pre-boarding area for our short hop to Sicilia, we were able to relax. Well, we tried. There is a lot of hubbub in these waiting areas and a young lady across from us carried on almost continuous phone conversations at the annoying volume these chats seem to require. Neither my sister nor I are blessed with a great deal of tolerance, so we spent our time suppressing the urge to snatch the phone out of the young lady's hand and fling it across the terminal.

Soon, but not soon enough, we were allowed to board the flight. When we reached our seats we learned that Patti's new seat mate was the one and the same young lady of phone chat fame. I found it slightly amusing. But again, by the time we landed in Palermo the winsome lass had endeared herself to my sister who even went so far as to take down the name of a pizzeria in West L.A! She intends to visit there the next time she's out that way.

Palermo

We landed on time in Palermo, made our way to the car rental place and located our car, a Renault. I hadn't seen a Renault since my good friend Steve and his wife Joyce drove a Renault Dauphine from Arkansas to Spokane, WA. on Steve's leave from March AFB in California. I was stationed at Fairchild, AFB in Spokane, Washington at the time but Terri and I were renting an apartment off base. They had bought the car new but none the less, by the time they were ready to leave, it had somehow lost oil and had to undergo major repair. Steve had to call his base and request a leave extension. I was hoping our Renault experience would be better than his.

We found the car, a nice compact hybrid hatchback. We loaded in our bags, I assumed the position behind the wheel, had just pushed the electronic ignition button and..... someone was blowing their horn at us!. We were warned that Italians are very impatient drivers but we were still in our parking space at the rental lot! Turned out to be a rental car employee who wanted to park a returned car in our spot. And away we went.

The car handled well and accelerated nicely when we hit the highway. The posted speed limit was seventy kilometers per hour and I got to about sixty before I noticed a car coming up behind me doing just a bit under the speed of sound. The driver showed no intention of slowing down or of passing me. He wanted me out of his way, or else. I moved gingerly to the right lane and he blew by like the roadrunner being chased by Wile E. Coyote.

According to our cell phone GPS, the hotel was approximately thirty-five minutes away. We followed the lady's instructions to the best of our ability and soon found ourselves hopelessly lost, heading toward who knows where. We pulled over and reconnoitered. We started out again: "Rerouting", she said. This turned out to be her favorite instruction and one that began to send chills down our spines. At one point we found ourselves in a quiet, rundown neighborhood. Three young men were strolling down the street so I pulled over and screwed up the courage to attempt communicating with them. They were good guys and really tried to make sense of my Italo-babble but we weren't getting anywhere. Then I said "Palermo, hotel in Palermo." At this, they looked at one another questioningly and, with a certain amount of empathy, "This is not Palermo. Palermo is back the way you came from." We had driven right through the city and into the next.

It got ugly there for a while. Patti was doing her best to communicate with "the voice" and I was doing my best to follow Patti's often unavoidable last second instructions. When we looked at our itinerary before the trip we were pleased to see there would be time to land, get a rental car, and find the hotel in daylight. It was now dusk and the sun was sinking fast into the Mediterranean. After more false starts and stops and countless re-routings we managed to find our destination in the dark. The thirty-five minute drive had taken us almost three and a half hours! But we were there.

Friday, 9/29/17

After a well earned night's sleep we wandered down to the complimentary breakfast. All but one of the hotels we stayed in were part of the same chain so regardless of how plain or ornate the building, the rooms were similarly arranged and the breakfast fare was from the same menu: fresh fruit; blood orange juice; two cereal choices; one cornflakes-like, the other crude bran. There were fresh slices of ham or cold, cured bacon, scrambled eggs (some with small hot dogs), an assortment of delicious pastries and, finally, a variety of coffee choices, none of them decaf. I know Italians are not big on breakfast so this was management's effort to appeal to travelers.

First on our agenda was to find the nearest post office and

to purchase international postage stamps. The desk told us we could find the local one just a couple of blocks down the very street we were on. It was an easy walk so off we went. The office was not yet open when we arrived. It was shortly after 9:00 AM but we figured, hey, we're in Sicily; the people here operate at a slower pace than we do. Soon, other pedestrians began to arrive. Some looked through the glass to see if anyone was in there. A while later an armored truck arrived and pulled up at the side door. Patti approached and asked if they were about to open. The man with the gun and a bag of something told her, "*Domani, domani!*", meaning, tomorrow! It was a weekday, not a holiday, and they were closed. When word spread to the people out front they shrugged it off and walked away. At home, there would have been armed insurrection!

Catacombe dei Cappuccini,

No, this is not where cappuccino coffee came from, nor do they serve it here. These catacombs were created by the Capuchin monks of Palermo when, in 1559, they ran out of room in their cemetery and began excavating the crypts below. The place itself looks mundane from the outside. It is located in a modest section of the city in a building that looks disturbingly like a small business establishment in a residential neighborhood, which may be why we, once again, drove around and around before realizing we were there.

The original intent was for the place to be used for dead friars. (You can pick them out by their elaborate garments, some with the ropes they wore as penance.) Capuchin Brother Silvestrio of Gubbio, was mummified and honored as the first person to be interred in the catacomb. Over the next two

Clueless In Paradise

centuries the monks accepted citizens of note and others who had the means to gain acceptance. Relatives could visit their loved ones and adorn their alcoves. There is a description of the process:

"The bodies were dehydrated on the racks of ceramic pipes in the catacombs and sometimes later washed with vinegar. Some of the bodies were embalmed and others enclosed in glass cabinets."

We were told the dehydration process could take two years. We also learned that prospective tenants were welcome to come to the place and pick out their location, even standing or lying in it to make sure of the fit. The catacombs were closed in 1880 officially, but there have been exceptions admitted from time to time. There are a reported 8,000 corpses and 1,252 mummies interred there. I will admit that after 30 minutes or so of strolling by the silent and sometimes accusing stares of the inhabitants I had had about enough. Patti, who has a remarkable fascination with this sort of thing, could probably have stayed longer.

As we reached the parking lot we saw a middle-aged man slumping against the front of the Renault. He had been walking around the lot when we arrived and was kind enough to point out a parking space. Now, we realized he was some sort of attendant whom we should have paid when we parked. In the nicest way possible he was there to collect from us before we left.

After a pleasant lunch in a nearby buffet-type restaurant we checked out of the hotel and hit the highway aiming straight for Realmonte.

Author's note:

Realmonte is a small town in the Agrigento province. As a young person, whenever I expressed interest in the genesis of my grand- parents I got information that was sketchy at best. I attribute this to the fact that all four were uneducated and may have had a poor knowledge of Sicily beyond the small communities in which they lived. And, they were all illiterate. Any information passed from them to my parents must be taken with a grain of salt. This much we know : Pasquale LaFranca, my maternal grandfather, when asked would reply, Agrigento. When we asked Grandpa Culotta, he said Palermo, the largest city in Sicily, but he was, in fact, from nearby Cefalú. As I recall, no one asked Grandma Anna where she was born. They were separated over half their lives so I know only that she may have come from Bagharia, a small city not far from Cefalú.

Realmonte/Agrigento

The drive to Realmonte was wonderfully uneventful. The GPS lady smiled on us and we arrived in good time. Our hotel was more than we could have dreamed. The Scala dei Turchi Resort was attractive, well maintained and ideally situated just across the road from the popular beach attraction for which it was named. Scala dei Turchi means "stairs of the Turks," so named, as legend has it, because of the stark white outcroppings that step down from shore into the water. It is believed this is where Turkish ships hid out from enemy warships.

Clueless In Paradise

We arrived in the early afternoon, checked in and strolled over to the bar. The nice fellow who spoke decent English but proclaimed his allegiance to the native Sicilian language, not the modern one, made us drinks. He gave me a knowing look as he poured a liberal amount of gin into Patti's tonic. I smiled and played co-conspirator; I didn't have the heart to tell him she is my sister, not my wife or girlfriend. It worked out better that way.

That evening we enjoyed a semi-formal dining experience in the resort's restaurant. The wine was an unpretentious red both tasty and refreshing. (I've always wanted to use "unpretentious" in a sentence about wine.) By the time we finished eating and drinking, the rigors of the first two days took their toll and sent us plodding along to our rooms for a well deserved rest.

Saturday, 9/30/17

I'm standing in the shade of a palm leaf, looking at the cool, clear azure water of the swimming pool while I wait for Patti to appear. I wonder why I didn't pack a bathing suit.

After breakfast we drove into the town of Realmonte, a real Italian village: narrow streets lined with apartments built some time long ago. There were those balconies where residents could stand and converse with visitors below. A young woman held up her new bambino or bambina so relatives parked in the street could get out and admire her or him. It was right out of a Vittorio De Sica movie. There was an open-air fruit and vegetable vendor at the crossroads in the center of town. I mention this because in our quest to locate the local cemetery in search of family crypts we passed it numerous times. After asking people along the streets for directions and even miming digging to get our message across, we found ourselves at the same place. in front of the fruit stand. On a side street we saw what looked like a mechanic's garage with two men working there. I sent Patti to ask them for help in hopes that a cute, little *Americana* of obvious Italian heritage could elicit better results than I could.

    A kind, elderly worker escorted her back to our car and in a combination of Italian, broken English and even a touch of German, (turns out he was Dutch and spoke both German and Italian!), broke our code and said "Ah, *cimitaro!* " (Pronounced *chimitaro* not *semitario!)* He asked us to follow him and proceeded on foot so we drove slowly behind. When he reached the top of the hill where we were to turn left he indicated I should follow him around the corner. A short block later, just across from that fruit stand, he signaled we should turn left again and there we would find the cemetery. To insure our ability to make the turn he put his hand out to stop a car that was about to enter the crossing. "Aspetta"! he told the driver, "Wait!" As we passed him we thanked him profusely: "Molte grazie, signor, molte grazie!" Sure enough, there was the cemetery, not a quarter of a mile from the crossroad we had passed numerous times.

    As cemeteries go, this one is beautiful. Row after row of beautifully constructed family crypts connected by shaded walkways. Many are adorned with floral arrangements, some ancient in appearance and long neglected by visitors. All were kept decent by maintenance workers. To our surprise there were numerous LaFranca family tombs, far more than we expected to find. Vellas and Zambito's, names familiar to us as friends and family. were also well represented.

Clueless In Paradise

But there were no Anselmo's, Grandma LaFranca's maiden name. This undermined our belief that my grandmother hailed from Realmonte and, instead, indicated that my grandfather LaFranca may have lived here rather than in Agrigento. Since we weren't able to visit the cemetery in the latter city, we can only guess as to why this is. It was a long way to go to find only more uncertainty.

The Valley of the Temples (Valle dei Templi)

The sun in the Valle dei Templi was hot that day, my friends, Africa hot! The Greek and Roman ruins are massive and amazing in their splendor. The highlight was the Temple of Juno, with its tall Doric columns. Its ruins lounge around like tattered yet stylish furniture. The temple and the accompanying structures were built by the occupying Greeks between 450 and 440 B.C.. They became a part of Roman culture during that empire's rule and were excavated and restored by an Italian archaeologist in the early 19th century. Many of the beautiful columns are streaked with red, scars left from the fires caused by the Carthaginian attack in 406 B.C.

Did I mention it was hot? By the time we had walked along the line of sites Patti and I were wrung out and ready to head back. Since I had failed to pack a bathing suit and since I was lusting to dip into the Mediterranean sea across the street from our hotel, we drove into Agrigento proper and visited a modern shopping center where I purchased a bathing costume. (I learned later I had left my credit card at the counter of the store. The desk clerk at our hotel called them but they had not found it.)

By the time we got back to our rooms the sun was low on

the horizon so we hustled down to the shore and walked around in the shallows. I never got the bathing suit wet but it was fun anyway. I did manage to get a great picture of the setting sun.

Sunday, 10/1/17

Siricusa

Refreshed by a good night's sleep and fueled by the standard breakfast fare, we bid a fond *arrivederci* to Scala dei Turchi and headed off for Siricusa, an ancient city near the southeastern corner of the island, known for its Greek and Roman ruins but most important to us, it was a convenient stop off on our way north to Taormina.

    The drive took us further inland than we had been so when we missed a turn, as we surely did from time to time, we were directed down rutted country roads bordered by tall growth. We had become inured to being off track and had begun enjoying the sites our wandering provided. Along one stretch of highway, we saw a stone wall that bordered farmland which stretched for a kilometer or more. (By now we were accustomed to thinking in metric terms.) The wall was made with large stones gathered from the surrounding area and were fitted together with no apparent bonding material despite their varying sizes and shapes. I like to think it was built in imitation of the famed Roman walls. Since I know no better, so it shall be. All in all, this turned out to be the least exciting and therefore the most enjoyable leg of our motoring experience.

Clueless In Paradise

We managed to find the city and our hotel with comparative ease. The Grand Hotel Villa Politi was grand indeed! This was the most elaborate of the lodgings we stayed in on our travels through Sicily. It was built in 1862 by Salvatore Politi, a famed Siricusan artist, and designed by his wife, Maria Teresa Politi, nee Laudien, an Austrian noblewoman who met and fell hopelessly in love with Politi. The hotel became a popular meeting place for the aristocracy and for people of fame and fortune. I may have tarnished a bit of the hotel's splendor by rat-a-tat-tatting my noisy bag across the vestibule.

The brochure reports with pride that the hotel "was used as a base by Winston Churchill during the allied invasion of Italy" Later, we had cocktails in the bar named after the great man himself. Other famous people to stay there include Pope John Paul II. The main room resembles something from a 1950's or 60's Technicolor movie. I expected to see Cary Grant stroll down the long staircase with Ingrid Bergman on his arm. A statue of Signora Politi occupies the center of a stone garden on the hotel grounds.

Our rooms, although nice enough, did not match the hotel's many splendors but we enjoyed being there just the same. It was while strolling around the nearby cafes and squares that we happened upon a delightful experience. Across the street from the hotel was a modern *pasticciria*, (pastry shop) that offered an array of foods ranging from the delicious to the sublime. But the real treat showed up as we were paying the cashier.

Into the shop walked an elderly lady whose bearing and charm bespoke a person of means and good breeding. She was short in stature, petite, well dressed and bore a remarkable resemblance to a dear friend of ours who passed away a few years ago. Just as we were registering her presence a young

Sam Culotta

waiter with a full tray of coffee and pastries stopped in his passage to greet her with the traditional two cheek kiss. In the process, he tipped the tray. The glasses and cups shattered on the tile floor, their contents spread across the entryway. We gasped, waiting for the recriminations to follow this *faux pas*. But there was only a look of understanding between the manager and the waiter. The lady's offer to pay for the damages was graciously refused.

Patti and I come from a family with old world ties. Our parents and relatives always showed great respect and affection for the elders among us. Witnessing this event we were filled with sweet melancholy. Almost all the members of that generation are gone from our lives and we missed them terribly at that moment. Which might explain why when we were paying to leave and found ourselves beside her we introduced ourselves as best we could. In the process, the lady indicated to Patti she should kiss her on each cheek, which she did. Before she could defend herself, I put my arm around her and kissed her forehead. I'm sure I crossed the line, but I just couldn't resist. Next morning we saw her again, this time walking from her lodgings to the *pasticciria*, and prevailed upon her to pose for a photograph. She may still be telling her *amici* about the well-intentioned *Americanos* who accosted her on her way to her favorite cafe.

The only sight-seeing we did in Siricusa was a short drive to the Sanctuary of the Mother of Tears, *Madonna della lacrima*. Named for the terra cotta sculpture of the Blessed Mother Mary which, on August 29, 1953 and continuing until September 1, 1953, wept tears. The tears were analyzed and determined to be consistent with human tears. A short three months later (surely a speed record for such matters) the event was declared a true manifestation of the Holy Mother.

Clueless In Paradise

In an October 17, 1954, radio broadcast, Pope Pius XII announced: "We acknowledge the unanimous declaration of the Episcopal Conference held in Sicily on the reality of the event." A few years later, in 1957, the Sanctuary was designed by two French architects.

The dimensions of the building are impressive. Suffice it to say, the modern structure is striking. It remains to this day the tallest building in Sircusa, covers an area of 4,700 meters and holds 11,000 people. We found it jarring amid all the ancient sites in the surrounding area but couldn't help marvel in its presence.

Monday, 10/2/17

Taormina

The drive to Taormina was longer than previous drives. Except for running into rain and passing through a series of tunnels carved through the hills and mountains it wasn't bad at all. These tunnels were dark in the truest sense of "being without light" and required all the illumination our little auto's headlamps could muster. By the third or fourth one of these I began to understand how a bat feels if a bat were traveling at high speed alongside some rather adventurous local drivers. The tunnels were very long and the roads curved, often leaving us with no sight of the proverbial light at the end of said tunnels. Each time we emerged from one we breathed deeply as if we had ascended from a deep sea dive. Yet we survived to enjoy the beauty of the area with one exception: our desire to see Mt. Etna was thwarted by cloudy weather. Imagine travelling all that way and missing the highest and most famous sight in Sicily.

A quick note about toll roads in Sicily: they are often unmanned so you're not sure it's alright to pass through the gate. The toll booth we reached at the entrance to the road to Taormina was attended by a young woman who looked like she just happened to be passing by and saw an opportunity to collect a few Euros. She was dressed in jeans, wore a nondescript lightweight jacket and was digging the sounds via an earplug attached to a cell phone. Never once did she make eye contact with us. The toll booth was in sorry condition and the faded signs were in Italian, so we had no idea how much to pay or where to stick the coins. She was nice enough to hold her hand out and take a moment to extract the correct amount... we hoped.

We were struck by the beauty of the mountainsides and the coastline of this picturesque area. Even with the clouds the scenery was spectacular. I can only imagine what it looks like on a bright sunny day because the weather was inclement both days we were there.

True to our tradition we managed to get lost looking for our hotel. It should have been a breeze since there was only one coast road, yet we found ourselves parked alongside the road in the rain wondering where the hell we were. Patti phoned the hotel and received directions. We started off again with renewed optimism. Then we stopped alongside the road in the rain, again, and Patti called the hotel, again. This time she learned that we were within a hundred meters of the place but hadn't noticed because there was a short, twisty, stone-paved road up an incline to the hillside resort. I became intimately familiar with this road the next day.

When we pulled up outside the entrance, the man who had been taking our calls awaited us at the door. He wore the expression of deep concern a father might have for his missing children. There was a palpable sense of relief among staff and travelers as we unloaded our luggage in the cozy hotel office.

The rain let up not long after we were settled in so we drove into the heart of the village for a little souvenir shopping and general gawking at the seaside sights. Later we found a very nice restaurant and settled in to a delicious dinner. Patti had pesto pasta and I had linguini carbonara. The wine choices were the standard Sicilian fare: vino rosso, or vino blanco. We chose the rosso and found it to be as good as it always was. My sister has a reliably smaller appetite than I have, so I was able to partake of her pasta as well as my own. Our server was warm and accommodating making the entire experience a pleasure.

Tuesday, 10/3/17

"Le Poste? Camminare per l' arcata!"

On the first day we were in Palermo we picked up a few postcards. Because the *Le Poste* was closed that day for no apparent reason, we were unable to purchase international postage stamps. Every day after that we managed to pick up a few more postcards but were never able to find a place to buy the stamps. A few leads proved to be futile because the vendors had local postage only. I wasn't all that distressed but my sister, renowned for her persistence and her almost

Sam Culotta

super human shopping skills, had this goal uppermost in her mind every day. Now we were in Taormina, our fourth, and penultimate destination and were still carting around postcards in need of stamps. The goal had been to get them in the mail soon enough for our families to receive them before we got home. We were fast running out of time.

Tired of driving around, we took a bus into the heart of the shopping area which featured a picturesque walking street lined with souvenir shops and open areas where people milled about with coffees and snacks. It was a tourist's dream come true. We did some shopping but kept an eye out for our most pressing need. When a post office did not appear, we asked a local vendor, using whatever language skills we had garnered in our short time in Sicily.

"Escuza, where is *Le Posta, prego."*

After a try or two we got an answer:

""*Le Poste? Camminare per l' arcata !, l' arcata!"*

The instruction was accompanied by a pointing of hands which indicated both the direction ahead and the shape of an arch. Sure enough, there was a lovely archway about a hundred yards away.

"Aha! Through the arch!" *Grazi, grazi.*

With renewed hope we resumed the hunt; there was a palpable sense that we were closing in on our prey. We crossed under the *arcata* with quickened pace. But alas, shop after shop, cafe after cafe, but no post office!

Clueless In Paradise

Our hopes fading, we enlisted the help of another local.

"Prego, Il Posta?"

"Camminare per l'arcata, l'arcata!"

"Encore" I thought! Again!

Another trek, another arch, another failure. Another local, another direction to go through *l'arcata!* By now we had covered almost a mile and had passed through two arches. Our hopes flagged, but what the hell else could we do? We walked, we passed through an arch and, we walked. The post office, when we found it, almost escaped our notice. It was not the edifice we are accustomed to but a modest, although modern, building not much larger than one of our Starbucks.

We entered, almost giddy with relief, and found there were a number of people in line and a few more people standing off to the side clutching small tickets with numbers. This was something with which we were familiar; easy, peasy, take a number and wait. I knew we were not in the U.S. because no one seemed the least concerned with waiting. Soon a woman, who must have been a supervisor, recognized us for the clueless *Americanos* we were. She took mercy on us, directed us to a window away from the crowd and turned us over to a postal clerk who had a good grasp of English. Within moments we left the post office with enough international postage to send all our postcards and any more we might gather in our remaining travels.

The postage crisis resolved, we moved on to souvenir shopping. It now became our most pressing concern. Patti had her own list to finish, but sweet sister that she is, she made sure to prod me toward fulfilling my obligations as well. I knew full well Terri had commissioned her to see to it I did right by my children, grandchildren and neighbors. And, I intended to get my wife something nice as well. We wended our way through the lanes, back through the arches, and not far from where the bus had dropped us off when it began to rain, lightly at first, and then heavy. It reached downpour status at one point and we, umbrella-less, were forced to take cover in the small doorway of a cafe with a group of fellow travelers. Some minutes later the rain lessened a bit and we decided to make a run for the bus. Alas, it had just left and wouldn't be back for twenty to thirty minutes. By now we were wet, tired and slightly irritated. (Speaking for myself, I would say well irritated.) Patti saw some cabs standing by and suggested we grab one.

    The cab ride cost us eleven Euros, a steal considering the conditions. It was a relief to be out of the rain and unconcerned with finding our way home. When we arrived outside the same door at which the friendly hotelier had met us the day before, we paid the cab driver, tipped nicely and prepared to dismount. As I gathered up my packages and belongings I lost my footing on the wet stones of the driveway. I didn't fall all at once but managed to do a balancing act worthy of Cirque du' Soleil, for a moment or two that is. I was wobbling toward the pavement when the driver grabbed my sleeve to keep me upright. He succeeded only in turning my ignominious descent into a slow-motion pratfall. For a finale I landed softly on my back in a large puddle of rain water. By this time I was laughing aloud at the absurdity of my situation. But not as loud as Patti was! Once I assured the driver I was uninjured, he felt it was safe to leave. In fairness to him, he held back his laughter at least until he was out of the driveway and on his way back to the cab stand where I'm sure he shared the story with his *amici*. I, on the other hand, had to sneak back to my room with soaked clothes and a laughing sister. Later, after a shower and a few drinks from the bar, my frame of mind, if not my dignity, was restored.

So, our stay in Taormina came to an end. Not until recently did I learn that despite the fame of the town of Corleone, most of The Godfather was filmed in this idyllic city. This is the way I learn most things: after it's too late to appreciate them.

Wednesday, 10/4/17

Cefalù

We took to the road with an extra fillip of anticipation. We were bound for Cefalù, land of our fathers, the Culotta clan. It would be the shortest leg of our drive around the Sicilian coast, the last stop before returning to Palermo for our final night. The drive was without drama unless you count stopping for a bite to eat at a casual eating place that reminded us of a truck stop restaurant on the roads through California. The lunch was not the problem, gassing up our rental car was. After failed attempts to get two different pay point computers to work, (one of which looked like it had been installed before the age of technology), I finally enlisted an attendant to do the honors the old fashioned way, manually. He misunderstood my instructions to pump twenty liters and pumped instead, twenty Euros. So we ended up with much less fuel than we expected. But at this point I just wanted to get away from the place.

The highway to Cefalù was the most modern we had been on. We buzzed along at a nice ninety to one hundred kilometers per hour passed occasionally by a Ferrari or Mercedes going a hundred and ninety or so. Along the way my sister saw a sign for a town named "Patti". Seriously. Of course we had to pull off and take a picture of her next to the pole holding the sign. We didn't go in to explore because we could see it was not much of a community aside from its remarkable name.

The sunny blue sky, the rocky coastline, the hilly landscape, the blue Mediterranean...beauty in every direction. It occurred to me that just now after days marked by periods of stress and moments of wonder, we were getting the hang of the place. Better late than never I suppose. As we approached Cefalù I hoped it wouldn't disappoint us. I had always imagined it to be a typical European village with an aura of old Sicily. I imagined our great grandpa Vincenzo taking his mules to blacksmith for shoeing. All quite bucolic.

It turns out that Cefalù has become one of the more popular resort areas in Sicily. It draws visitors from all over Europe as well as from the Arab countries and North America. The core of the old city remains but the entire shoreline with its fine sand beaches and stunning rock formations are a great draw; it was still busy with the last wave of summer visitors. We drove into the busier part of the town and began our search for the hotel we had reserved. Before we had gone more than a block we came face to face with a large, modern shop front announcing "Culotta Macelleria" (Culotta Butcher Shop). We vowed to visit it once we were settled in to our lodgings. There was the usual difficulty finding the hotel and then finding a place to park. The hotel was a resort just across the street from the beach with its beautiful blue umbrellas and chairs and the typical beach restaurants and cafes. Honestly, it was more than we could have hoped for considering our lodgings were chosen by our travel agent for their locations and a minimum of three star ratings. (Most were four star rated actually. Kudos once again to Natalie at AAA!)

After we freshened up we took to the road again and went straight to the Culotta meat market. I know it doesn't sound glamorous but remember, our great grandfather raised army mules. a nice butcher shop is a giant step up the economic ladder. The entrance featured one of those beaded curtains such as you see in Moroccan Kasbahs. Maybe evidence of the Arab influence on Sicilian life. The owner had just wrapped and delivered some meat to a customer when we arrived. Once we were alone with him we announced our name and told the man a little about our family's past in his fair city. He was a very nice fellow somewhere around sixty I would venture. After some pleasant conversation we were forced to accept the fact that it was impossible to determine if some of his kin had emigrated to America around the time ours had. Before we left he told us there was a restaurant on the beach very near to our hotel that was owned and operated by a Culotta family. With hope renewed, we thanked him and bid him a fond *buongiorno.*

We found the beach restaurant with no trouble at all. We were hot and tired and getting hungry so this was an opportunity to kill three birds with one stone. The proprietor's son was running the place when we arrived and introduced ourselves as "the Culottas from America". He was very pleased to meet us and even stopped what he was doing to sit down with us for a chat. Everything went well; the father came in at one point and the son introduced us to him. He wasn't as impressed, but he was polite.

    We talked about our families, looking for a connection somewhere. Then the young man asked the fatal question: "How do you spell your name?" When we told him I could see his bubble pop. "Oh, he said, ours is spelled Colada." We had been pronouncing our name in American. Culotta is actually pronounced "Cool Lot- Ah" in Italian. I knew this, of course, but our family had always used the Americanized pronunciation, probably to avoid sounding too foreign. In fact, I used Colada myself when I wanted to simplify the spelling for reservations or phone messages. Our almost relative found the whole thing amusing and offered us a nice table for our dinner. Any hopes of a free dinner vanished. But he was solicitous and made sure we had the very best service.

    After another fine dinner, we decided to take a long stroll along the strand. By now it was dark but the walkway was well lit and populated by locals as well as tourists. The cool evening air off the sea was just what the doctor ordered for two travel weary, well fed *Americanos*. It was nice to see a few people with dogs, a sight I did not realize I missed until then. It was a short walk to the hotel where we spent a very comfortable night.

Thursday, 10/5, 2017

The last full day of our adventure. We walked to the central part of town to finish up our souvenir shopping and take in the sights. The coastline here is comparable to that of our Northern California coast. There are steep cliffs that end in large rocks which stir up the otherwise modest Mediterranean waves. This is the rocky coastline that confronted Sicily's first king, Roger II, on his return from the Italian mainland in the early twelfth century. His ship was storm tossed and in danger of foundering on the rocks. Legend has it, he knelt down on deck and vowed to God to build a great cathedral on the high promontory of Cefalù if he and his crew were spared. They were spared and King Roger was true to his word. Construction of the *Duomo Basilica* began in 1131 and towers above all surrounding structures.

The cathedral itself is magnificent and the surrounding area features a public square lined with shops selling souvenirs and food. There were more than a few young people, some lovers, sitting on the steps that lead to the cathedral entrance. Again, I couldn't help thinking of all the European movies I've watched, envious of being there. We spent some time in the church itself then walked down into the square. There was a nice shop that featured an amazing selection of gelato flavors. We each got one to eat as we walked around looking in the shops and taking in the atmosphere. This was not the most adventurous or dramatic day of our trip but it was certainly one of the most pleasant and satisfying. I felt perfectly at home in this city of our fathers and would love to visit it again.

Then it was back to our hotel to check out, load the car again, and make the relatively short drive to Palermo for our final night's stay in Sicily.

Palermo, Encore

I'm sorry to report that our final visit to Palermo was no more pleasant than our first. We stayed at the same hotel, but this time the air conditioning was not working and our rooms were on the fourth floor, a floor they reserve for people they don't like, I suspect. They were small, seedy and poorly lit. The guest must insert the room card into the wall receptacle to allow lighting in the interior, such as it was. But just when said guest became involved in anything that required illumination, the lights went out and the card had to be reinserted. I'm sure this was done in the service of energy preservation but it just made for an uncomfortable and annoying situation. The single bed looked and felt like an army cot. It brought back unhappy memories of my time in Air Force basic training.

    Patti and I went to the lounge area and sat on the balcony with drinks to escape the heat. The traffic noise and engine exhaust were not pleasant but it did beat being in our rooms. We planned to get up early the next morning to give ourselves time to get lost on the way to the airport. We would need time to turn in our rental car and queue up for our flight. We enjoyed our drinks and headed back to our cells.

    I decided to exact a small measure of revenge for the paucity of illumination by over indulging in water. Rather than stuff myself into the small shower designed for pygmies,(God forbid you should drop the soap; you might crack your skull bending to pick it up.) I filled up the tub for a long soak Due to the water restrictions in California we seldom take tub baths, so this would be my only luxury. I enjoyed every moment of it as I swished around with abandon and refreshed with hot water every few minutes. It was the only pleasure that final night offered.

    My sister and I inherited a family trait from our father: Punctuality. Nay, more explanation is in order, the noun punctuality requires an intensifier: "Compulsive" works. It goes beyond just being on time because of the compulsive quality. We are not only punctual we are also unreasonably horrified at the thought of not making it to somewhere like an airport in time to drop off a rental car and check in for our flight. We share this debility but Patti suffers from it more than I.

Our Al Italia flight to Rome was scheduled to depart Palermo at 7:55 AM. We figured we needed to be there only an hour or so before time. But we had the rental car to return, and we knew there was a high risk of getting lost on the way there even though traffic would be light. For this reason (and more) Patti wanted to check out of the hotel and be on the road by 6:00 AM. She figured that to do this we should get up by five A.M. Her anxiety and intensity over the matter told me further negotiation was futile. I've been married long enough to know when to quit. We arranged for one or the other of us to call the other at 5:00 AM. "just in case," and retired for the night.

Friday, 10/6, 2017

I managed to sleep most of the night despite the humidity and army cot bed. I awoke well before 5:00 AM and called Patti immediately, just in case. She answered almost before the phone rang. Not surprising at all, she had hardly slept. But now we were awake and the hounds were released: the race was on.

It was dark. The hotel seemed abandoned but for one groggy desk man who must have drawn the short straw. He proved to be capable and even courteous, no easy task under these conditions. I know I would have been the last person on earth the hotel would want dealing with departing tourists at this time of morning. He helped us out with our bags and walked with us to the parking lot behind the building. Because of the hour he had to unlock the gate to let us out.

We turned on to the main street and headed for home comforted by the last minute directions we got from the desk man. We were sure this lessened the chance of our driving off into parts unknown never to be seen again. The traffic was very light which made it so much easier to follow signs and correct errors. The instructions said that we should turn at a certain street in a certain direction and that would pretty much be it! Couldn't be much easier than that.

That certain street was not where it was supposed to be. Mild anxiety nosed its way into our comfort zone. Soon, it was apparent we were no longer on the simple route to our intended destination. But fear not, we still had our GPS. The voice of Our Lady of Re- routing was back. After a few route adjustments, which caused a small amount of perspiration to gather under my arms, we seemed to find ourselves back on the right road and then on to the highway headed toward the airport. It was a wonderful feeling.

Merrily we sped along in the dark; I drove and Patti watched for signs. Just as we were feeling confident we came to a turn-off that could have been the one we needed, or maybe not. Before we could process this information the turn-off was behind us and we were zooming down an almost empty highway. We couldn't turn back because there were no exits for miles. To add salt to the wound, we drove past what was certainly the airport runway; its lights stretched back toward the terminal. Anxiety ruled once again. Within minutes we saw the looming black presence of a mountain. It looked like it sat right in the middle of the highway. "This is it", I

Clueless In Paradise

thought, "*ciao* fair world." Before we could say our Acts of Contrition, an exit appeared. We took it, knowing it could get us back on the highway and to the exit we missed. We would be OK. We would go home after all.

    Surprise! We had to circle the airport twice before we found the rental agency. But find it we did. We un-lugged our bags for the umpteeth, but not last, time, ditched the Renault, wandered around for a while before we found the car key drop box and then hurried into the terminal. After we checked in our bags we joined a group of fellow travelers heading for the gate. The line to board was already formed. "See?" my sister said, "We darn near missed the flight! This is why I wanted to leave so early!" I just smiled sheepishly and told her she was right. A few minutes had passed when suddenly Patti said: " Oh, God! This isn't even the gate for Al Italia!" We took off at a fast walk, scurried for what felt like miles to the other end of the terminal and found the right gate. They were boarding as well. It seemed we were incapable of going from any point "A" to any point "B". By now we were so exasperated all we could do was laugh breathlessly.

We landed in Rome in plenty of time to make our connector flight to Los Angeles with no further dramatics. The flight home seemed to take far longer than the one to Rome ten days earlier. For one thing, the huge Boeing 777 faced headwinds the entire way which made for a slower and more turbulent ride. For another, we were tired and more than ready to be home again. The food was not good at all. There were a few items we couldn't identify as fish, fowl or plant. And whatever it was, it was tepid. Many of the passengers seemed surly, especially the one in the seat ahead of me. Seems he didn't like the way I tapped the controls on the consul attached to his backrest. Instead of asking me nicely to avoid hammering the thing, he turned and scolded me. I realized my error but didn't appreciate his aggressiveness. As though my silent curse had been heard, he suffered a maddening series of impositions for the remainder of the flight through no fault of mine.

    Not all the passengers were grouchy; my sister's new seat mate was a nice lady who became her third and final temporary best friend. She was returning from a very romantic tryst with a man she met on Match.Com. Turns out her third marriage had ended not too long ago and she was searching for male companionship. Her new paramour was quite a guy. He was so smitten by her internet personality and accompanying photos that he flew her to Rome where the two of them romped and frolicked in many chic venues. Much of the travel was by yacht. She was so happy and she couldn't wait to tell Patti all about it. As if on cue, she whipped out her trusty i Phone and subjected my captive sister to an astounding number of pictures of her beau, his adult sons, his friends, her family, her friends and many of the places they visited.

    Something you should know about my sister: she can't stand looking at cell phone photos so this had turned into her own personal circle of Hell. I was glad to be in the aisle seat because not only did I not have to view the photos, I was free to chortle quietly. Patti handled herself admirably well, never doing more than casting a tortured sideways glance my way. This was small payback for the pleasure I provided her with my flat-tired luggage bag.

    And so it went. I watched two movies, played video games, worked my crossword puzzle and, when all else failed, tried to sleep. Alas, sleep was impossible. Once again, the endless stream of restless passengers careened up and down the narrow aisle dislodging my arm from its resting place with eerie consistency. My only pleasure was the Sicilian one of justice because the guy in front of me was bothered over and over by a woman in his row with a bladder problem who needed to use the facilities. The grump never grumbled though, probably due to his Italian deference to *La Donna*.

Friday, 10/06/17

Honey, I'm Home

Arrival time at LAX was on the same day we left Rome; we had re-gained the day we lost. Disembarking takes a long time when there are 220 exhausted passengers. They had to find their shoes, purses, carry-on bags; they had to unwind from the cramped seats to full extension, a painful process in many cases. They had to pull their luggage out of overhead bins, luggage that often grazed the skulls of those of us waiting patiently to get up. Finally, we were able to join the herd and short step our way down the aisle to the exit ramp. Patti's newest friend said she had a connector flight to San Diego so we were destined to part at some point. That point wasn't yet. She seemed to take a special interest in our progress, maybe because we reminded her of her parents.

We were not exactly at the terminal yet. First we had to board a bus so long it was hinged in the middle, making it look like a gigantic caterpillar. Passengers were stuffed together, each gripping their personal belongings. I was put in mind of old black and white photos I've seen of poor immigrants in the

Sam Culotta

holds of ships. This must be what our grandparents looked like when they queued up to file onto Ellis Island. People close enough to share their gum tried hard to avoid staring into one another's eyes during the long ride to the main terminal.

With what remained of our energy, we managed to drag our luggage to the next station. The end, after all, was in sight. All that remained was to clear customs, claim our baggage and find the shuttle that would take us home. Near the end of the flight we were given forms to fill out stating what we were bringing into the U.S. from Italy. "Oh, cool" I thought, "this will make getting through customs easier. But when we got there we were routed to a line of computer terminals and directed to fill out an electronic questionnaire that asked the same questions we had answered on the paper form.

We finished, and as we were walking toward the next check point, Patti told me she had inadvertently marked the wrong box at the bottom which asked her to verify that her information was correct. I assured her there was no problem since we were moving along fine. When we filed through the next check point the guard pointed to the right line for me and to the left for her. Oh, oh. I stopped at the exit to wait for her but she was nowhere to be seen, so I figured we'd meet up at luggage claim. Oddly enough, my baggage and hers were among the first to arrive, a complete reversal of every other time I've claimed baggage after a flight. Patti had still not arrived so I pulled both bags off the merry-go-round and stepped away to wait for her.

I became concerned when Patti failed to show up in what I considered a reasonable amount of time. I hoped she was not looking for me somewhere else. My cell phone, on cue, proved to be useless in the terminal for some reason, so I couldn't call her or receive her call. The situation was getting more worrisome by the minute. Then I saw her waving to me from across the way. Turns out she was peeled off the line because of the discrepancy on her customs survey. Thankfully, she hadn't been strip searched.

Again, we trudged with our luggage to the area outside the doors where we were to pick up our shuttle service. And again, my big bag with the flat wheel made that machine gun sound which drew unsolicited attention. By now I didn't care. I was hot, thirsty, tired and not a little irritated. When we got to the shuttle area we learned we had just missed ours and it would be thirty minutes or more before another one going to our area would arrive. Forty-five minutes or so later, we climbed into the van with a huge sigh of relief. We had made it. Barring a flat tire or hijacking of the shuttle we would be home soon.

Debriefing

I got out of the shuttle and walked over to Terri, took her in my arms and made her promise to not let me go away again. But already, in the short time we've been back we remember less the tribulations than the pleasures. Difficulties are a part of any travels whether by plane, train or automobile. We don't feel we did much worse than any other inexperienced world traveler. In retrospect, there were many things we wished we had done differently, many places we should have visited, many things we should have done, but to do so would have required another week or two. Our main purpose was to visit the places in which our family were born and lived their early years. Secondarily, we wanted to see as much of Sicily as we could. We succeeded in the first but failed in the second to some degree. You can't flit from city to city in eight days and see everything you should. And it wasn't our fault the traffic in Palermo was hellish or that clouds hid Mt. Etna or there were no street vendors selling grilled lamb intestines on a skewer.

We did eat canoli, we did step into the Mediterranean Sea, we did see the family tombs of people with our family names. We met people who seemed aloof at first but were always helpful and considerate. (not counting the guy in the seat in front of me on the flight home). And we met a sweet lady in Siricusa who reminded us so much of our late friend and of how much we miss the loved ones of her generation. We almost mastered the infamous Sicilian road system including the much feared and often encountered roundabouts. We did this all without having an accident or doing noticeable damage to our rental car.

We drank fine wine, ate well and often, and didn't get *aggitta* once. Most of all, we were fortunate enough to take in the breathtaking beauty of the island of Sicily, more picturesque than the pictures can show. We visited a cathedral built in the early 13th Century. We saw ruins of ancient Greek and Roman temples dating from the fourth century B.C. And we walked the paths our ancestors trod. We saw narrow cobblestone streets our grandparents may have played on, even heard the loud greeting of a lady from the street up to a new mother and her baby on a veranda.

We did just fine, my sister and I.

Final note: The first thing I did when I got home was empty out that large suitcase with the flat wheel and stuff it into the trash barrel. *Basta!*

Acknowledgments

I wish to thank my wife, Terri, my daughter, Denise and my son, James for encouraging me to accept my sister Patti Amesbury's offer to join her on the trip to Sicily. Their combined efforts got me off the couch, onto a plane and over the ocean to the land of our fathers.

Special thanks to Patti for being co-pilot and navigator in our often chaotic wanderings, and for her hard work editing this book and for Terri's re-editing of our edits. Be assured, any flaws that remain are solely the fault of the author.

Made in the USA
Middletown, DE
30 March 2019